POVERTY, VULNERABILITY, AND FISCAL SUSTAINABILITY IN THE PEOPLE'S REPUBLIC OF CHINA

JUNE 2021

ASIAN DEVELOPMENT BANK

ADB

CONTENTS

TABLES, FIGURES, AND BOXES

FOREWORD

In 2009, the Ministry of Finance (MOF) of the People's Republic of China (PRC) asked the Asian Development Bank (ADB) to create an ADB-PRC Knowledge Sharing Platform (KSP)—to promote South-South cooperation. We knew ADB would be an excellent partner in promoting evidence-based learning between the PRC and other developing member countries. In 2012, we signed an agreement with ADB for a Regional Knowledge Sharing Initiative—to synchronize resources and improve our knowledge sharing. That way, we could contribute to the conceptualization, design, and financing on important emerging development issues. Given the KSP's role as regional knowledge broker, the PRC and ADB could closely align the knowledge work with the strategic priorities of ADB's Strategy 2030 and Country Partnership Strategy (CPS), aiming at building a network for knowledge-sharing, promoting dialogue, and strengthening the cooperative partnership between the PRC and the other developing member countries.

This report is testament to our KSP cooperation. It recognizes the PRC's achievements in poverty reduction and provides an in-depth analysis of the PRC's practice and experience in eliminating absolute poverty and promoting fiscally sustainable development. Three case studies on poverty reduction in Guangdong, Hunan, and Yunnan provinces are also included. Meanwhile, this report proposes policy recommendations for the PRC to address education, health care, and care for the growing number of elderly in the PRC.

In preparing this report, ADB and the MOF held two workshops and a seminar in 2020. First was the Poverty Reduction and Sustainable Development Interim Workshop on 29 April to discuss the initial research outline. Participants were mainly researchers and report authors. The second was the Poverty Reduction and Sustainable Development Review Workshop on 11 August, where initial findings were shared for the various chapters of the poverty reduction study. And a third virtual seminar on Poverty Reduction and Sustainable Development on 29 September presented the research findings, including the provincial case studies.

In March 2021, the ADB Board of Directors adopted a new CPS, pointing the way for the next steps of utilizing ADB's financial and intellectual resources to promote green and sustainable development in the PRC. We expect that the insights in this report will serve as one of the outcomes of knowledge cooperation in the new phase of both sides' cooperation, helping the PRC implement its 14th Five-Year Plan, further promoting institutional building, and forming a new pattern of "Dual Circulation" development.

Cheng Zhijun
Acting Director General
Department of International Economic and Financial Cooperation
Ministry of Finance
People's Republic of China

FOREWORD

The People's Republic of China (PRC) has a long and successful record of poverty reduction and alleviation, the result of sustained rapid economic growth and a strong commitment to anti-poverty policies. When reforms began in the late 1970s, more than 80% of the population lived in absolute poverty. Balancing economic growth with social and macroeconomic stability was critical to the PRC's success. Yet, there remains a need for a post-2020 anti-poverty strategy—one that targets reducing "vulnerability" to poverty. This report looks closely at vulnerability.

Vulnerability is the likelihood an individual's or household's well-being will fall below a socially acceptable benchmark. Ensuring growth is inclusive creates new economic opportunities available to all segments of society. If development becomes more inclusive, it reduces the size of the vulnerable population. This report targets four specific vulnerable groups: (i) the vulnerable elderly; (ii) young children of rural migrants; (iii) the rural population and rural-to-urban migrants; and (iv) those whose access to health care is jeopardized by rapid urbanization and aging.

When setting anti-poverty policies and programs, fiscal sustainability is critical. The report explores policies that improve the quality of life of vulnerable groups, but do not necessarily require excessive fiscal support. It also describes how restructuring government expenditures can meet strategic priorities while maintaining fiscal sustainability, with private sector participation if needed.

The government's response to the coronavirus disease (COVID-19) pandemic included several immediate measures to help vulnerable groups. Medium- to long-term policies will likely remain focused on revitalizing the rural sector and strengthening rural-urban linkages. The report suggests that a holistic approach will lead to better prioritization, better balancing macroeconomic stability with social progress. The historical experience of the PRC bodes well for the future.

M. Teresa Kho
Director General
East Asia Department
Asian Development Bank
Manila, Philippines

ACKNOWLEDGMENTS

This report is the product of a study of East Asia Department (EARD) of the Asian Development Bank (ADB) on the context for a post-2020 poverty reduction strategy. The support and guidance of Acting Director General Cheng Zhijun; Director General for the World Bank Group and ADB Qiangwu Zhou; former Director General Zhongjing Wang; and then Deputy Director General and currently an Executive Director to Asian Development Bank Weihua Liu (all from Ministry of Finance, the People's Republic of China), and former Director General James Lynch and current Director General M. Teresa Kho of EARD throughout production is gratefully acknowledged.

Staff from EARD prepared this report; led by Akiko Terada-Hagiwara, Principal Economist of Office of the Director General, who coordinated the production of the publication, assisted by Sophia Castillo-Plaza. Technical and research support was provided by Maria Cynthia Petalcorin and Imelda Baleta.

Several authors contributed to specific sections. Subsection coordinators included Akiko Terada-Hagiwara for fiscal sustainability; Shingo Kimura for rural development; Najibullah Habib for social public spending; and Li Xu together with Zhao Jiuling from Yunnan, Deng Weiping from Hunan, and Yu Wanbing from Guangdong for the provincial case studies.

Three review workshops were held. The study team warmly appreciates the reviewers of the background papers that contributed to this study. Those include Xiaoqin Fan; Dahai Sun; Sangay Penjor; Eisuke Tajima; Suzanne Robertson; Liping Xu; Naoyuki Yoshino; Shenggen Fan; Rana Hasan; Karin Schelzig; Yi Jiang; and Yuebin Xu. Wendy Walker, Amir Jilani, and Meredith Wyse reviewed the entire report, and provided valuable comments. Tian Min of PRC MOF coordinated the review by ministries in the PRC.

Josef Yap conducted an economic review and edited the manuscript. Guy Sacerdoti edited the manuscript, Lingfen Li translated to Chinese, and Longyun Peng and Dongni Jia reviewed the Chinese manuscript. Joe Mark Ganaban typeset the manuscript. Cleone Baradas prepared the abstract cover design. ADB's resident mission in the PRC supported the production of the report, and ADB's Department of Communications supported the publication and dissemination of the report.

This publication was financed under TA 8997-PRC: Promoting Partnerships for South-South Cooperation II.

CONTRIBUTORS

Naoyuki Yoshino is Professor Emeritus at Keio University, Japan, and former Dean and CEO of the Asian Development Bank Institute. He is also the Director of the Japan Financial Services Agency's Financial Research Center, and Chairperson of the Meeting of Japanese Government Bond Investors.

Guoqin Zhao is associate researcher of Research Institute of Finance and Economics, Central University of Finance and Economics, Beijing.

Shenggen Fan is Chair Professor at the College of Economics and Management and Dean of the Academy of Global Food Economics and Policy at China Agricultural University.

Akiko Terada-Hagiwara is Principal Economist at the Office of the Director General of the East Asia Department, Asian Development Bank.

Jinhua Wu is former Director at the Provincial Finance Department, International Financial Cooperation Office, Guangdong Province.

Haixiang Xiao is Associate Professor of Public Finance at the School of Economics and Trade, Hunan University, People's Republic of China.

Tiwei Zhang is Professor at the Institute of Rural Development, Yunnan Academy of Social Sciences, Yunnan Province, People's Republic of China.

Wusheng Yu is Professor at the Department of Food and Resource Economics (IFRO), University of Copenhagen, Denmark.

Mingxi Han is PhD student at Renmin University of China, People's Republic of China, and is currently a visiting PhD student at the University of Copenhagen.

Shingo Kimura is Senior Natural Resources and Agriculture Specialist at the Environment, Natural Resources and Agriculture Division of the East Asia Department, Asian Development Bank

Yuebin Xu, is Professor at the Institute of Advanced Studies in Humanities and Social Sciences, Beijing Normal University.

Wei Ha is Deputy Dean, Graduate School of Education, Peking University.

Najibullah Habib is Health Specialist at the Urban and Social Sectors Division of the East Asia Department, Asian Development Bank.

ABBREVIATIONS

ADB	–	Asian Development Bank
APSD	–	Assistance for People with Special Difficulties
CCCPC	–	Central Committee of the Communist Party of China
CNY	–	Chinese yuan
COVID-19	–	Coronavirus disease 2019
CPC	–	Communist Party of China
EARD	–	East Asia Department
FDI	–	foreign direct investment
GDP	–	gross domestic product
GTAP	–	Global Trade Analysis Project
HCBC	–	home and community-based care
ICT	–	information and communication technology
IMF	–	International Monetary Fund
kg	–	kilogram
KSP	–	knowledge sharing platform
MCA	–	Ministry of Civil Affairs
MOF	–	Ministry of Finance
MPS	–	moderately prosperous society
NBS	–	National Bureau of Statistics
NDRC	–	National Development and Reform Commission
NHC	–	National Health Commission
NPC	–	National People's Congress
PPP	–	public-private partnership
PRC	–	People's Republic of China
PSD	–	people with special difficulties
RBPS	–	Residents Basic Pension System
RC	–	residential care
SARS	–	severe acute respiratory syndrome
UEBPS	–	Urban Employees' Basic Pension System
WHO	–	World Health Organization

EXECUTIVE SUMMARY

In February 2021, the People's Republic of China (PRC) officially announced it had eradicated absolute poverty. The long and challenging 40- year journey to eradicate poverty succeeded.

Its success was the result of sustained rapid economic growth and a strong commitment to effective anti-poverty policies. The PRC is now the world's second-largest economy and its largest merchandise exporter. Annual per capita growth in gross domestic product (GDP) rose to 8.2% in the 1980s, 9.3% in the 1990s and 2000s, and 6.8% in 2011–2019. When reforms began in 1978, more than 80% of the population lived in absolute poverty. By 2019, it had declined to less than 1% (ADB, 2020a). This is equivalent to 850 million people escaping absolute poverty—accounting for about 70% of worldwide poverty reduction during this period.

This book examines the need for a new poverty strategy in the PRC. As an upper middle-income country with no absolute poverty, a single, fixed monetary threshold for income or consumption poverty may no longer adequately reflect deprivation. Thus, the PRC's post-2020 poverty reduction strategy will (i) treat poverty as multidimensional; (ii) reinvigorate rural development; (iii) develop an integrated rural-urban poverty strategy; and (iv) address the vulnerability of certain segments of the population to avoid falling back into poverty.

Vulnerability refers to the likelihood that an individual or household will experience a level of well-being that falls below a socially acceptable standard. Ensuring growth is inclusive creates new economic opportunities and makes them available to all segments of society. Thus, inclusivity and vulnerability are inversely related. If development becomes more inclusive, it reduces the size of the vulnerable population. Based on the main demographic drivers of socioeconomic structural transformation, four specific vulnerable groups are identified in this report: (i) the elderly; (ii) young children of rural migrants; (iii) the rural population and rural-to-urban migrants; and (iv) those whose access to health care is jeopardized by urbanization and population aging. Vulnerability can be reduced; but this requires a comprehensive set of policies and fiscal support, largely through public goods and services.

Balancing economic growth with social and macroeconomic stability was one of the critical factors that led to the PRC's success. Over the last 4 decades of rapid socioeconomic structural change, fiscal policy has been critical. In particular, anti-poverty policies were clearly reflected in government spending priorities. However, population aging, urbanization, and slowing economic growth either reduce or overextend fiscal resources, diminishing the amount of public goods and services available for vulnerable groups. Population aging also reduces the efficacy of fiscal policy, requiring more fiscal resources to replicate the effects of previous stimulus packages. Further, the coronavirus disease 2019 (COVID-19) pandemic complicated both the country's fiscal position and vulnerability to increased poverty incidence. The hardest hit were rural migrant workers, many trapped in their hometowns due to lockdown policies. An estimated 175 million full-time jobs were lost in the first quarter of 2020 with 26.2 million more through June. Small and medium-sized enterprises were also badly affected. Higher food prices, lower incomes, higher unemployment, and lower remittances to rural and urban households led to a rise in poverty incidence, using a $4.9 poverty threshold (Zhang, Diao, and Chen 2020). An estimated 4.8 million rural and urban remittance-receiving households (about 14.4 million family members) fell into poverty during the lockdown.

An important question for policymakers is what level of social services and protection should be financed by the state, and how much should be shouldered by individuals and households. The PRC needs to strike the appropriate balance between its own capabilities and the availability of other resources. It needs to avoid the type of fiscal crisis faced by many advanced countries, arising in part from unsustainable entitlement programs.

This report recommends policies on how the PRC can simultaneously reform its fiscal system to ensure fiscal sustainability and mitigate the risks faced by vulnerable groups. These include policies that (i) alter the composition of government expenditures—to meet evolving strategic priorities while maintaining fiscal sustainability, such as higher allocations for social and environmental public investment and recurrent expenditures, or allow resource reallocation over time from lower- to higher-priority government programs; (ii) improve the efficiency of revenue mobilization, for example, by changing revenue structures; (iii) reform intergovernmental fiscal relations by better aligning available resources with expenditure responsibility at different government levels ; and (iv) strengthen the management of government finances and improve the efficiency of public expenditures, which includes enhancing private sector participation. This will improve the quality of life of vulnerable groups, but does not necessarily require fiscal support.

For policies to protect the specified vulnerable groups, the report offers several recommendations: (i) for the elderly, the PRC must create adequate fiscal space before aging progresses too far—the current elderly care system needs to better integrate and balance home and community-based care (HCBC) with residential care (RC), with financing priorities reoriented (based on research) to prepare for a dramatic increase as people with a single child enter old age; (ii) young children of rural migrants— early childhood development must continue to be part of a national health, education and poverty alleviation strategy, with policies more comprehensive and equitable, and focusing on rural poor children and their caregivers; (iii) the pandemic showed that rural-to-urban migrants are vulnerable, and that short-term policies can help returning rural migrants cope with economic shocks—examples include the distribution of unemployment benefits along with financial and other assistance for starting new businesses (with special attention given to preventing vulnerable groups from slipping into short- or medium-term poverty); and (iv) those whose access to health care is jeopardized by urbanization and population aging—to offer more complex, high quality forms of health care associated with higher levels of income and education. The PRC recognizes the important effects health has on income, employment, schooling, and social interaction. The Healthy China 2030 program uses a participatory approach to promote better health care and a healthy environment. In addition, the response to the pandemic exposed both the strengths and weaknesses of the PRC health-care system. Aside from the major components of the new poverty strategy, the pandemic may lead to a reassessment of where the vulnerability of certain groups intensifies or new vulnerable groups are created.

Case studies from three provinces—Guangdong, Hunan, and Yunnan—provide useful insights on how fiscal policy was effectively used for poverty and vulnerability alleviation. The Guangdong case study focuses on measures that can enhance the efficacy and efficiency of spending programs. The Hunan case study describes how spending programs are directed at specific vulnerable groups. And the case study of Yongsheng County, in Yunnan Province, describes general measures to improve efficacy and efficiency as well as specific programs that address poverty and vulnerability.

Despite rising rural per capita income, persistent urban-rural income disparities continue relative to high-income countries. In 2020, average per capita income in urban areas remained 2.6 times higher than in rural regions. Agriculture, farmers, and rural areas (three *nong*) comprise the core government policies for the country to become a moderately prosperous society (*xiao kang*) by closing the income gap. Hence, this report discusses a holistic strategy to reduce vulnerability and achieve sustainable development.

The 2018 Rural Vitalization Strategy adopts a wider approach to promote integrated rural development. The PRC invested heavily in network infrastructure in rural areas—including roads, the telephone system, and in providing internet access. It connected farmers to markets and enabled manufacturing and service industries to develop. Beyond providing a platform for transactions, e-commerce platforms invested in logistics and marketing infrastructure in rural villages and provided training for farmers to adopt these new technologies. Reinvigorating rural development through leasing out farmland can generate opportunities to boost off-farm incomes, reduce vulnerability, and narrow the urban-rural income disparity. Off-farm income now accounts for more than 70% of rural household income compared to 25.6% in 1990.

Integrated rural-urban development ultimately requires continued reform toward universal provisions of basic public services—such as education, employment opportunities, old age care, health care, and housing (with or without *hukou*). Although the disparity within the basic public service between urban and rural residents has narrowed over time, there remain restrictions related to *hukou* registration. Allowing labor to freely flow between urban and rural areas not only contributes to narrowing the rural-urban income gap, but would also attract human capital to rural areas.

A more comprehensive agri-environmental policy—coupled with more investment in rural environmental infrastructure—could provide incentives for more sustainable production. Developing the rural "experience" through ecotourism would diversify sources of farmer incomes and create additional employment opportunities in rural areas.

CHARTING SUSTAINABLE POVERTY REDUCTION POST-2020 AND COVID-19

1

Poverty Reduction in the People's Republic of China

Rapid economic growth in the PRC and effective anti-poverty policies eradicated absolute poverty in 2020, from 80% before 1978.

The People's Republic of China (PRC) has a long and successful record of poverty reduction, the result of sustained rapid economic growth and a strong commitment to anti-poverty policies. Economic growth followed the introduction of market-oriented reforms and the opening up policy. Annual per capita growth in gross domestic product (GDP) rose to 8.2% in the 1980s, 9.3% in the 1990s and 2000s, and 6.8% in 2011–2019. The PRC is now the world's second-largest economy and largest merchandise exporter. Rapid growth of manufacturing exports and inward foreign direct investment (FDI) has helped make the PRC a leading manufacturing center in the world. Increasingly, the country's growth is supported by indigenous innovation. Rapid growth has also reduced poverty and improved living standards. When reforms began, more than 80% of the population lived in absolute poverty. By 2019, it had declined to less than 1% (ADB 2020a). In February 2021, the government announced it has succeeded in eradicating absolute poverty.[1] This is equivalent to 850 million people escaping absolute poverty—or about 70% of worldwide poverty reduction during this period.

Meanwhile, balancing economic growth with social and macroeconomic stability was one of the crucial factors that led to the PRC's success (World Bank 2013). The government applied a mix of fiscal, administrative, and employment policies to maintain social stability during this period of rapid economic and structural change. In particular, anti-poverty policies were reflected in government spending priorities (Figure 1). National general public budget education expenditure as a proportion of GDP rose from 1.8% of GDP in 2000 to 3.9% in 2012, before declining to 3.5% in 2019; expenditure on health rose from 0.5% in 2000 to 1.7% in 2019, peaking at 1.8% in 2016; and expenditure on social security and employment rose from 2.0% in 2007 to 3.0% in 2019. Other expenditure items related to inclusive development show similar trends.

Even with absolute poverty eradicated, it is important to note that the national poverty line is more than 40% below the threshold income to qualify for minimum living standard guarantee payments (*Dibao*) (NBS: Poverty Monitoring Report of Rural China 2019; Ministry of Civil Affairs). Once the median poverty line among upper-middle income countries is used, the poverty rate (in 2016) increases to 24% (World Bank 2020).

---

[1] Unless otherwise noted, this report uses the official PRC definition of absolute poverty—a rural poverty line of CNY2,300 (Converted to 2011 purchasing power parity, it is approximately equivalent to US$2.3 per person per day) or less per year (in constant 2010 values).

Figure 1: Selected Fiscal Data
(% of GDP)

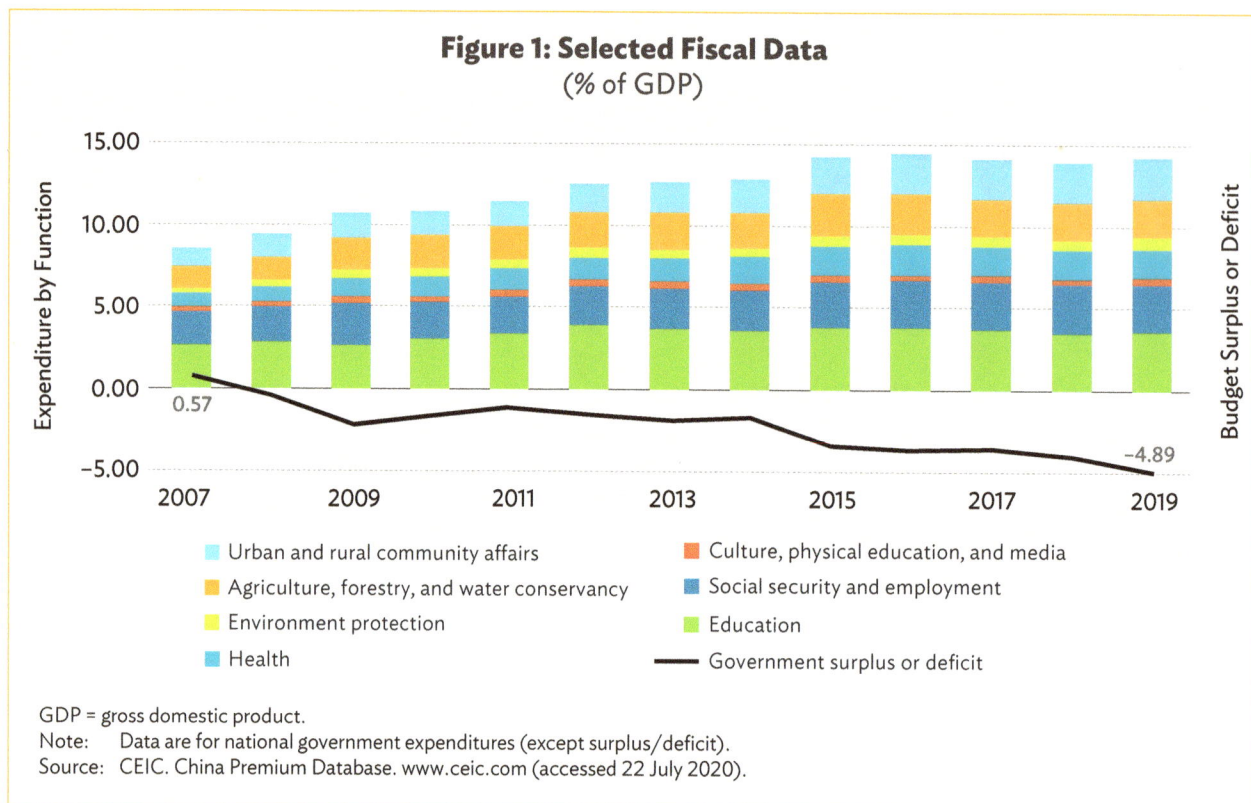

GDP = gross domestic product.
Note: Data are for national government expenditures (except surplus/deficit).
Source: CEIC. China Premium Database. www.ceic.com (accessed 22 July 2020).

At high GDP per capita levels, experience shows that countries continue to have segments of their populations struggling with deprivation; although the nature of deprivation may be different than before. For these countries, a single, fixed monetary threshold for income or consumption poverty may no longer adequately reflect deprivation. The PRC is no exception. This concept of what constitutes deprivation increasingly depends on norms that evolve with rising standards of living. One aspect is that individuals must have sufficient resources to meet higher societal expectations—regarding standards of nutrition, housing, and health care, among other things.

Need for a New Poverty Strategy

The PRC must adopt a new poverty strategy to respond to higher living standards and address the vulnerability to poverty of certain segments of the population.

Development transforms economies and societies in many ways. It is manifested in urbanization, population aging, structural reallocation from agriculture and manufacturing into services, shifting from low to high value-added technologies, and slowing GDP growth. The PRC's poverty strategy will need to adapt to these quantitative and qualitative changes.

With these considerations in mind, the PRC's post-2020 poverty reduction strategy will need to be reformulated to focus on the following areas: treating poverty as multidimensional; reinvigorating rural development; developing an integrated rural– urban poverty strategy; and including vulnerability in poverty alleviation policy. This report deals mainly with vulnerability.

Vulnerability can be reduced; but this requires a comprehensive set of policies and fiscal support, largely through public goods and services.

Development is usually accompanied by expanded public sector capacity. This makes possible increases in the provision of public goods, expanded social programs, improvements in public security and legal and regulatory systems— all of which can promote inclusive development. It can be defined as development that creates new economic opportunities and widens access to those opportunities for all segments of society.

Inclusivity and vulnerability are therefore inversely related. If development is more inclusive, it reduces the size of the vulnerable population. For reasons to be explained later, this report focuses on four specific vulnerable groups and recommends policies on how to mitigate the risks associated with their vulnerability: the elderly—recognizing that the PRC is an aging society; young children of rural migrants; the rural population and rural-to-urban migrants; and those whose access to health care is being jeopardized by the phenomenon of urbanization and aging.

Vulnerability, Inclusive Development, and Fiscal Sustainability

Fiscal policy has been an important part of the PRC's drive to become a high-income country. By efficiently mobilizing and spending around 30% of GDP, the government can increase availability of crucial public goods and services,

address key externalities, and support a rise in overall efficiency (World Bank 2013). Government has a central role to play in reducing inequalities in opportunity—protecting vulnerable groups and maintaining macroeconomic and financial stability. Well-designed fiscal reform can help sustain growth, address important social gaps, and make development more environmentally friendly.

Some areas of fiscal reform are particularly relevant to the current situation; (i) the composition of spending must be adjusted to reflect changes in government functions, as the country reaches higher income levels and priorities shift toward social and environmental objectives; (ii) the balance between macroeconomic stability, economic growth and greater social and environmental sustainability must be maintained; and (iii) intergovernmental fiscal arrangements should be equitable—both vertically (between levels of government) and horizontally (across jurisdictions), especially at the sub-provincial level. This will allow the adequate provision of local infrastructure, social protection, and basic public services (World Bank 2013).

As the PRC modernizes its economy, it needs to develop a vision, core values, and guiding principles that will support inclusive development (Lee et al. 2020). An important question for policymakers is what level of social services and protection should the state aim to finance, and how much of the responsibilities should be shouldered by individuals and households. The government has to be circumspect over its role. After averaging 1.3% of GDP from 1990–2014, the budget deficit (defined as the difference between fiscal revenues and expenditures) jumped to an average of 4.0% during 2015–2019, reaching 4.9% in 2019 (see Figure 1).[2] The PRC needs to strike the appropriate balance and avoid the predicament that many advanced countries currently face—a fiscal crisis arising in part from financially unsustainable entitlement programs.

---

[2]   Following the revision of Budget Law in 2015, the fiscal balance would include items such as social security and transfers to and from stabilization fund. Based on this definition, the average fiscal balance was 2.6% for 2015-2019, and reached 2.8% in 2019.

Population aging, urbanization, and slowing economic growth either reduce or overextend fiscal resources, diminishing the amount of public goods and services available for vulnerable groups.

This report examines two important aspects of the PRC's structural transformation—population aging and urbanization—primarily due to their impact on fiscal sustainability. Population aging leads to a decline in the proportion of the working population, in the long run reducing output and aggregate consumption if no actions are taken. This reduces available fiscal resources, as does an aggregate deceleration in economic growth. Meanwhile, while urbanization has an overall positive effect on economic growth, the influx of rural migrants has led to additional demand for social services. Foremost is support for "left-behind children" in terms of education and nutrition. Other areas that require government support for migrants are housing, social insurance, and job training.

Overextension occurs when the same amount of resources are used to serve a larger group. Allocating more resources to preserve the same level and quality of service may not be feasible if fiscal sustainability is to be maintained. There are three general options available to maintain the same level and quality of service. One is to increase government expenditures to cover the additional requirements while simultaneously generating more revenue to prevent a widening of the fiscal deficit. The second is to improve the efficiency or productivity of the service-provider. The third option is to attract resources from outside government, which usually means the private sector. This is the general approach taken in sections III–VII.

Population aging also reduces the efficacy of fiscal policy, requiring more fiscal resources to replicate the effects of previous stimulus packages.

Policymakers must be mindful of the impact an aging population has on the efficacy of macroeconomic policy. Empirical studies show that population aging weakens the effectiveness of fiscal and monetary policies, largely due to a decline in labor supply. During recessions, a larger fiscal stimulus package would be needed to support aggregate demand, which would require maintaining larger fiscal space to allow for wider swings in the fiscal position (Honda and Miyamoto 2020). Furthermore, given the weak effect fiscal stimulus has in boosting output, even during recessions, other macroeconomic tools or structural reform measures would have to play a more important role.

The Impact of the COVID-19 Pandemic on the Vulnerable

The coronavirus disease 2019 (COVID-19) pandemic complicated both the fiscal position and vulnerability by causing the economy to contract and increasing poverty incidence.

To control the spread of the virus, many governments worldwide partially or fully closed their borders and restricted people's mobility.

In many instances—the city of Wuhan being the prime example—lockdowns were imposed. The outbreak began in December 2019, but the impact was not felt until 23 January when a lockdown was declared in Wuhan. This occurred just before the PRC New Year. As is tradition, producers, processors, retailers, wholesalers, and many households had stored food for at least 2 weeks prior to the celebration. Thus, the immediate impact was small. But as more provinces began to introduce lockdowns, physical distancing, restrictions on the movement of people and food, urban district and rural village management was disrupted. Schools were shut. Non-essential economic activities were shut—

including transportation, construction, factories, restaurants, cinemas, and entertainment parks. February 2020 was the most difficult month in the PRC for people's livelihoods and the economy (Fan, Si, and Zhang 2020).

As a result, the economy suffered a triple blow. Initially, transport and labor restrictions impaired production capacity, disrupting supply chains. It reduced demand with people locked down and workers laid off. Air travel restrictions and border closures limited both the movement of people and goods across borders. The rapid rise in unemployment and underemployment led to a sharp reduction in purchases of nonessential goods. There was also the fear of a potential financial shock, as rising nonperforming loans added stress on banks and other financial institutions. The sudden stop in economic activity and workforce mobility greatly affected the poor and vulnerable—childless seniors, orphans, the disabled, unemployed, and rural migrants, among others. For example, there were 290.8 million rural migrant workers in 2019— 116.5 million working in counties and 174 million in cities (NBS 2020). By February 2020, the number had decreased to 122.5 million, with 54 million less than the number year on year due to the impact of pandemic. The economic disruption channeled mainly through the food supply chain, leading to a decline in agricultural trade and rising food prices. Groups previously not vulnerable were also adversely affected— such as food suppliers (Zhang et al. 2020).

Quantitative estimates of the impact—using the GTAP model—show that the extent of economic downturn depends on how long it takes to contain domestic virus outbreaks.

Early in the pandemic, ADB simulated the potential economic impact of COVID-19 using the Global Trade Analysis Project (GTAP) model—a multi-region computable general equilibrium model (ADB 2020b). It measured the increase in trade costs (those affecting global supply chains, people's mobility and tourism), the supply-side productivity shock (that cuts wages and corporate earnings, reducing consumption and investment) and fiscal stimulus through various macroeconomic policy instruments. It estimated the impact of COVID-19 in 2020 would be from $5.8 trillion to $8.8 trillion—or 6.4% to 9.7% of global GDP. A critical COVID-19 impact is on labor. Globally, the GTAP analysis suggests that the equivalent of 158 million to 242 million jobs will be lost. In the PRC, an estimated 5 million people lost their jobs in the first 2 months of 2020. Wage incomes would also fall globally, with the estimate ranging from $1.2 trillion to $1.8 trillion. The comparative figures for the PRC were $253 billion and $386 billion. This has a significant impact on poverty incidence.

Objective of the Report: A Strategy to Reduce Poverty and Sustain Development

The main objective of this report is to recommend policies that reduce the vulnerability of specific groups and lead to sustainable development.

This report describes a possible new poverty strategy for the PRC. The rationale is detailed in section II. The discussion covers the strategy's major elements— treating poverty as multidimensional, reinvigorating rural development, developing an integrated rural-urban poverty strategy, and including vulnerable groups in poverty policy. Vulnerable groups include the rural population, the elderly, young children, minorities, persons with disabilities, and persons with inadequate human capital. Putting a face on vulnerability allows policy responses to be more readily designed. A general overview is presented in the last part of this section.

The critical role public goods play is described in section III, including the crucial issue of ensuring adequate fiscal space. Two drivers of vulnerability—population aging and urbanization—have a significant impact on fiscal space, possibly overextending resources, as mentioned above. An obvious policy option would be to increase resources through taxation, for example, or repurpose resources from other categories such as infrastructure to social spending. However, these alternatives are not central to this report.

Sections IV, V, VI and VII discuss the key elements of the new poverty strategy. Apart from areas that will require fiscal resources, the discussion also deals with policies that reduce vulnerability without adding pressure on fiscal resources. Greater efficiency of existing service providers including social organizations and private sector participation are considered crucial.

Section IV takes a deep look into rural poverty and how it can be mitigated using an integrated rural-urban poverty strategy. Sections V–VII examine elderly care, human capital development (focusing on early childhood education), and access to health services. Each looks at the three general options to mitigate vulnerability, described earlier.

More details on the pandemic response can be found in the discussion on health care. The report recognizes that the COVID-19 pandemic may have exacerbated the situation facing existing vulnerable groups. And it may have even created new vulnerable groups. A new poverty strategy must at the very least anticipate the contours of a post-pandemic world. Section VII also takes this into account.

VIEWING POVERTY IN THE PEOPLE'S REPUBLIC OF CHINA UNDER A NEW LENS

2

Rationale for a New Poverty Strategy

Justifying a new poverty strategy is primarily a matter of explaining the rationale for each major component.

In this section, the description of each component offers a rationale for its inclusion in the new poverty strategy. As mentioned, the components include (i) treating poverty as multidimensional, (ii) reinvigorating rural development, which encompasses (iii) an expanded rural-urban integration strategy, and (iv) clarifying the concept of vulnerability with regard to poverty. Vulnerability is discussed in sections II.2 to II.4.

Treating Poverty as Multidimensional

Measuring poverty should expand beyond a monetary poverty line to incorporate indicators that can be more usefully analyzed using a dashboard approach.

Poverty should be redefined from being unidimensional to being multidimensional. The monetary poverty line remains an important indicator, but should be supplemented systematically by incorporating additional indicators that capture important dimensions of deprivation—those more relevant to upper-middle-income countries. They include those with particular attention to concerns related to capabilities, inclusion and exclusion, and people's subjective assessments of what it means to be poor. These concerns imply the need for indicators that capture not only outcomes, but mechanisms and processes as well.

Many relevant indicators are nonmonetary, with some being relative in nature. Examples include objective measures, such as years of schooling, internet access, and height-weight ratio. Others are more subjective, such as perceived safety, one's self-assessed health, and perceived loneliness. Further study is needed to identify the set of supplementary indicators most useful for the PRC at its current stage of development. Adopting a new poverty line and adding indicators may require investment in new data collection and statistical work.

Multiple dimensions of poverty can be analyzed using a dashboard approach—or combined in a multidimensional poverty index. Both approaches have been used by other countries to specify policy targets and develop policies that promote inclusive development. Malaysia, Mexico, and South Africa use multidimensional poverty indexes. Canada uses a monetary poverty line augmented by a dashboard of other indicators—including measures of food insecurity, unmet health care and housing needs, literacy, numeracy, youth engagement and asset resilience (Employment and Social Development Canada 2018). From a policy perspective, the dashboard approach has the advantage of clearly identifying the dimensions of poverty requiring the most attention.

This chapter draws on the background papers prepared by ADB's Resident Mission in the PRC (ADB 2020c) and Shenggen Fan (Fan and Zhang 2021).

Figure 2: Relative versus Absolute Poverty Rates
(%)

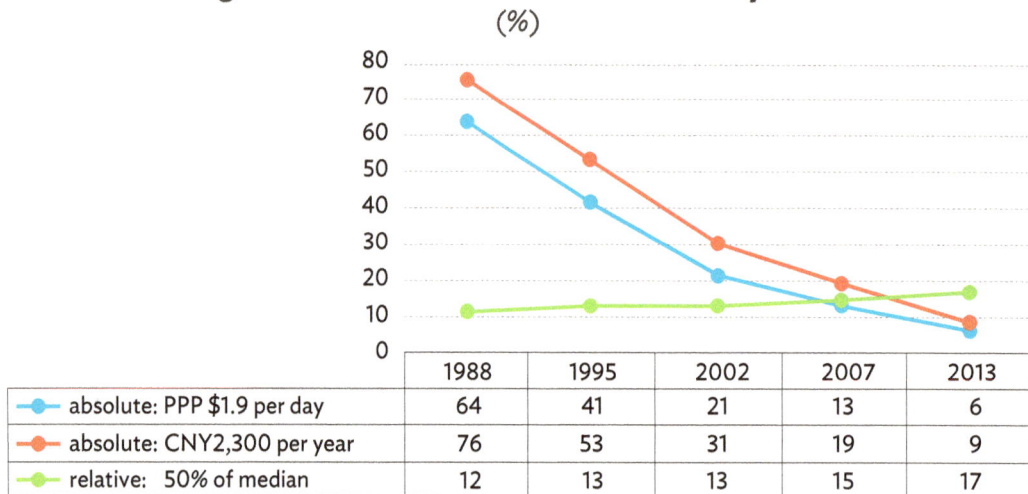

	1988	1995	2002	2007	2013
absolute: PPP $1.9 per day	64	41	21	13	6
absolute: CNY2,300 per year	76	53	31	19	9
relative: 50% of median	12	13	13	15	17

PPP = purchasing power parity, PRC = People's Republic of China.
Notes: Calculated using CHIP survey data. The absolute poverty lines are the international PPP $1.9 per day and the PRC's official
          poverty line of CNY2,300 per year. The relative poverty line is 50% of median rural household income per capita.
Sources: S. Li, P. Zhan, and Y. Shen. 2020. New Patterns in China's Rural Poverty. In T. Sicular, S. Li, X. Yue and H. Sato, eds. *Changing
          Trends in China's Inequality: Evidence, Analysis, and Prospects*. New York: Oxford University Press.

Reinvigorating Rural Development

The strategy to address rural poverty must be more holistic and account for migrants entering urban areas.

Rural areas have been central to the PRC's poverty reduction strategy. However, rural reforms, rural to urban migration, and general economic development resulted in rising rural per capita incomes. In more recent years, non-agricultural income—such as wage income—has become an important driver of rural income growth. However, per capita income of rural residents still lags far behind their urban counterparts, despite some narrowing of the gap in recent years. Moreover, the regional rural income imbalance remains between the more affluent eastern region and the central and western regions. The new poverty strategy has to explore other areas to promote rural development. Some of these would be rural land rights reform and land market development, agricultural modernization, expanding basic rural services and safety nets, promotion of rural tourism and the non-agriculture sector, and protection of the rural environment—all important components of an integrated rural-urban strategy.

Developing an Integrated Rural-Urban Poverty Strategy

Thus far, the PRC's poverty reduction efforts have justifiably focused on rural areas. But now more than half the population is urban, and this share will continue to rise.

Urbanization brings new forms of vulnerability and disadvantage. Similar to many other countries, rural-to-urban migrants are particularly at risk. The primary reason in the PRC is the *hukou* (household registration) system, which leads to the difference of people's equal access to basic public services, such as child education, health care, and housing. Steps have been taken to reform the *hukou* system—for example, towns with less than 1 million permanent residents lifted *hukou* restrictions. But more restrictions need to be lifted.

Urban poverty has other distinct features that require new programs. One is the difficulty of finding affordable housing, visible in increasing homelessness, inadequate or low-quality housing (including poor sanitation and water), insecure (rental or informal) housing, and remote housing in peripheral areas. Because designing effective housing interventions for the poor is difficult, further work is needed to identify successful programs and adapt them to specific situations in the PRC.

Rapid urban expansion has dislocated people and disrupted social networks, resulting in isolation and an increasing lack of informal family, social, community and economic networks. The loss of these networks can increase vulnerability to poverty and exclusion, especially for the elderly and disabled, and sometimes for families with young children. An important component of any urban poverty policy is to find ways to promote social cohesion and inclusion. This can be done by providing free public spaces, such as parks and libraries, offering low-cost cultural and social activities, and supporting citizens, communities, and volunteer organizations develop these activities.

Including Measures That Address Vulnerability

The new poverty strategy centers on vulnerability as it helps identify specific segments of society that require more focused policy interventions.

With absolute poverty officially eradicated, poverty policy should shift from lifting people above the poverty line to keeping people from falling back into poverty. Many households in the PRC, both poor and non-poor, lack economic security. Poverty studies find that households with these problems typically constitute a disproportionate share of the poor, and are particularly vulnerable to shocks such as the COVID-19 pandemic.

Defining Vulnerability and Its Relationship to Poverty

Vulnerability refers to the likelihood that at some time in the future an individual or household will experience a level of well-being that falls below a socially acceptable level (Hoddinott and Quisumbing 2010; Gallardo 2018; Haughton and Kandker 2009). Vulnerability can occur in multiple dimensions of well-being—for example, in nutrition, housing, or employment. This report focuses on vulnerability to poverty, but similar concepts and methods apply to other dimensions of vulnerability.

Various factors cause vulnerability. Households face risks associated with illness, disability and death that cause loss of earning power or unanticipated, catastrophic expenses—due to natural disasters, for example. Job loss is an important risk that can occur from temporary economic fluctuations or long-term shifts in the economy associated with structural and technological change. Structural change in the PRC has led to the reallocation of employment in the informal and services sectors, where jobs are often part-time and temporary. Technological change can cause job losses due to skill obsolescence and job displacement.

Vulnerability to poverty refers to the likelihood of being poor. For those not poor, vulnerability to poverty means being at risk of becoming poor. For those who are poor, vulnerability to poverty means being at risk of falling deeper into poverty. Vulnerability to poverty is the combined result of two factors: (i) a household's expected (or mean) income and (ii) its exposure to risk. For example, households that are not poor but have incomes close to the poverty line can be vulnerable to poverty even if they face only a small amount of risk. Households farther from the poverty line can also be vulnerable to poverty if they face large, high-probability risks that would cause a substantial drop in income.

Vulnerability to poverty differs among groups and across locations. The literature on poverty often refers to "vulnerable groups," such as minority ethnic groups, women, children, the disabled, and the elderly. In principle, the term "vulnerable group" should mean a group that has a relatively high probability of being poor. In practice the term is often used loosely. In devising policies to help vulnerable groups, it is important to identify whether their vulnerability arises due to low expected outcomes, the presence of uninsured risks, or a combination of both. These different sources of vulnerability require different policy responses. To the extent vulnerability arises from the presence of risks, it is important to identify the types of risks that underlie that vulnerability. The types of risks can differ substantially among groups. For example, rural households will be vulnerable to adverse weather events that affect farm incomes, while urban households may be more vulnerable to macroeconomic shocks that cause employment loss or inflation.

All these considerations create challenges for governments in monitoring and addressing vulnerability to poverty. The relationship of vulnerability to poverty is complex. The challenges are conceptual as well as practical. They can arise due to low expected consumption, risk, or a combination of the two. Policies must address the underlying sources of vulnerability. For example, vulnerability due to low expected consumption will require different types of policies than vulnerability due to risk—and different types of risks require different policies.

The methods commonly used to measure vulnerability, however, do not provide the needed information and often lag behind the research. The gap between practice and research creates an opportunity for improvement. Adopting more effective methods to analyze vulnerability can support the development of more effective and efficient policies to address the issue. But first, we need to know what vulnerable groups look like.

Characteristics of Major Vulnerable Groups

This report focuses on the vulnerability and risks of four specific groups: (i) the elderly; (ii) young children of rural migrants; (iii) the rural population and rural-to-urban migrants; and (iv) those whose access to health care is jeopardized by urbanization and aging.

The choice of groups is largely based on the main drivers of structural transformation—an aging society and urbanization. A large share of the elderly reduces labor supply and adds to the resources needed for social security. Urbanization largely involves rural migration, a process that has revealed the weaknesses of the *hukou* system. Apart from *hukou* reform, complementary policies for dealing with left-behind children, housing, and employment training should also be designed and implemented. However, one aspect that can reduce the divide in living standards between rural and urban areas is a reinvigorated rural development strategy. Also, an aging society and urbanization strain the health-care system.

The Elderly

In 2020, the "China Development Report: trends of population aging and policies" (Xiaohui 2020) projected that by 2022, people over age 65 would account for 14.0% of the population—with the share nearly doubling to 27.9% by 2050. Early on, the government focused on establishing social security systems and expanding coverage from pensions and medical care insurance. Social assistance was designed as a safety net for families falling into poverty. It was only in the early 2010s when increasing emphasis was placed on developing an Elderly Care system.

Apart from low income and pensions that constrain access to adequate care, elderly people are vulnerable due to various factors, such as high prevalence of chronic diseases, mental disorders, functional impairments, poverty, reduced availability of informal care, and inadequate housing, among others. Poverty among the elderly has been a persistent phenomenon. By the end of 2020, there were 3.7 million rural and 0.2 million urban elderly receiving Assistance for People with Special Difficulties (APSD), and 1.5 million urban and 13.4 million rural elderly receiving *Dibao* (minimum living provision) benefits—accounting for 18.4% and 37% of the *Dibao* recipients, respectively. This means there were 22.7 million elderly living in poverty, or around 9% of the population aged over 60.

An aging population has important implications for fiscal policy. To keep pace with the increase, pensions are estimated to rise from 2.3% of GDP in 2010 to nearly 4% in 2020 and 6% by 2030 (World Bank 2013). If pension coverage is expanded to cover all rural and urban informal workers, then the requirement jumps to nearly 10% of GDP by 2030. Meanwhile, Honda and Miyamoto (2020) find that as population ages, the output effects of fiscal spending shocks weaken. They also find that, while high-debt countries generally face weaker fiscal multipliers, high-debt aging economies face even weaker multipliers. These results point to important policy implications—that population aging requires larger fiscal stimulus to support aggregate demand during recessions, and thus requires larger fiscal space to allow for wider fiscal swings without threatening fiscal sustainability. Given the larger longer-term needs for social expenditures in aging economies, countries should prepare to create significant fiscal space before aging progresses too far.

Early Childhood

Since the opening-up and reform period began, the PRC has seen the most massive migration from rural to urban areas in the world, with an estimated 288.4 million rural laborers moving to cities to seek jobs as of 2018 (China Yearbook of Household Survey 2019). This rural-urban migration led to a geographical segmentation of rural families with one or both parents working in cities. As a result, the children left behind have become the main concern for child development in poor rural areas.

The response was a new urbanization policy to promote universal access to essential public services in both urban and rural areas. The provision of basic services in many cities thus began to include the rural migrant population. Consequently, many rural parents looking for urban jobs now choose to take their children with them to receive compulsory education in cities. However, preschool children still have difficulties in entering urban kindergartens. As a result, even in cities, raising preschool children remains a family burden. Thus, children left behind in rural areas are more likely to move to the city with their parents after reaching the age of compulsory education, while children aged below 6 years are more likely to stay in rural areas with aging grandparents.

Improving the quality of human capital entering the future labor force remains a key anti-poverty strategy. Thus, early childhood development must be part of a national health, education and poverty alleviation strategy.

Rural Poverty

Rural reforms led by the household responsibility system during the 1970s gave a tremendous boost to agricultural productivity and increased farm income. On average, rural household income increased by 11.9% per year during 1990–2019. In contrast, urban household income rose by 12.4% annually during the same period.

Despite rising rural per capita income, persistent urban-rural income disparities continue. This income gap is quite large relative to high-income countries. PRC low-income rural populations receive large amounts of government minimum income assistance.

Significant income disparities also exist across rural income groups. The lowest quintile of the rural population had average annual disposable incomes of CYN1,067 in 2005, which was set as the official rural poverty line in 2008 (Table 1). By contrast, rural residents in the upper middle-income group had incomes three times higher, with incomes for those in the high-income group six times greater.

Access to Health

The PRC recognizes the important effects of health on income, employment, schooling, and social interactions. The Healthy China 2030 program uses a participatory approach to promote better health care; significantly expands the health-care industry; establishes a sound health promotion system for physical, social and economic well-being; and aims to create a healthy environment.

A major challenge is to offer more complex, high quality forms of health care desired by those with higher levels of income and education. The government increased health expenditures from CNY359 billion ($50.2 billion) in 2008 to CNY1.5 trillion ($212.6 billion) in 2017. Health expenditure as a share of GDP increased from 4.6% in 2000 to 6.4% in 2017. These health-care reforms and investments have resulted in near universal health insurance coverage.

Reduced mortality and fertility led to a rapidly aging society, while the social and economic transformation increased urbanization. In 2018, the United Nations reported that 55% of the world population lived in urban areas, and was expected to increase to 68% by 2050. In the PRC, the urban population increased from 17.9% in 1978 to 59.2% in 2018. This coincided with the demographic transition, with about 20% of the urban population projected to be over 60 years old by 2030. Many will reach very old age and require specialized health care to maintain well-being and quality of life. The World Health Organization estimates 24% of the global health burden stems from the consequence of living in urban environments. Infectious diseases, such as COVID-19, spread rapidly in dense urban areas.

Taken together, aging, urbanization, and population density make the PRC relatively more susceptible to both disease spread and its consequences. Aging weakens the immune system and is related to increased susceptibility to both non-communicable diseases (such as diabetes, heart disease and cancer) and communicable diseases (such as influenza). Massive, rapid urbanization has significant public health implications, with urban crowding and urban sprawl inadvertently changing land use. Migrants dealing with a new environment and new behaviors, conditions, and frequent

Table 1: Annual Disposable Income per Capita of Rural Residents by Income Group
(CNY)

Sector	2005	2008	2011	2014	2017	2018	Average annual growth rate (2005–2018)
Poverty standard		1,067	2,300				
Low income (20%)	1,067	1,500	2,001	2,768	3,302	3,666	10.23%
Lower middle income (20%)	2,018	2,935	4,256	6,604	8,349	8,509	11.84%
Middle income (20%)	2,851	4,203	6,208	9,504	11,978	12,530	12.16%
Upper middle income (20%)	4,003	5,929	8,894	13,449	16,944	18,052	12.35%
High income (20%)	7,747	11,290	16,783	23,947	31,299	34,043	12.11%

CNY = Chinese yuan.
Sources: For income information: China Yearbook of Household Survey. 2019. For poverty standard: Poverty Monitoring Report of Rural China. 2016.

contact expose them to unfamiliar microbes, generating new health threats. These health risks are aggravated by the *hukou* system, with its limited access to health-care services.

Vulnerability Related to the COVID-19 Pandemic

Rural migrants are one of the hardest hit groups.

Actual data show that GDP in the first quarter of 2020 contracted by 6.8% and by 1.6% in the first half of the year. Although this was above earlier forecasts, employment is estimated to have decreased by 175 million full-time jobs in the first quarter and 26.2 million in the second. Hardest hit were rural migrant workers, many held up in their hometowns due to lockdown policies (Zhang et al. 2020). Small and medium-sized enterprises, which account for 80% of jobs, were also badly affected.

The average wage rate of the rural migrant workers declined by 7.9% in the first quarter. Even as most migrant workers returned to the cities in the second quarter, the average wage dropped by 6.7%. Higher food prices, lower incomes, higher unemployment, and lower remittances to rural and urban households have led to an increase in poverty incidence. For example, using a higher CNY7,500 per year ($4.9 per day equivalent) relative poverty threshold (Zhang, Diao, and Chen 2020), an estimated 4.8 million rural and urban remittance-receiving households—equivalent to 14.4 million family members—fell back into poverty during the lockdown.

The pandemic response showcased both the strengths and weaknesses of the PRC health-care system. Aside from the major components of the new poverty strategy, the pandemic may lead authorities to reassess where the vulnerability of certain groups intensifies or new vulnerable groups are created. Regardless, there are certain development themes that can reduce exposure to vulnerability.

Inclusive Development Helps Address Vulnerability

A comprehensive set of inclusive development policies reduces vulnerability to poverty.

Inclusive development creates economic opportunities and widens access to those opportunities; so all segments of society can participate (Ali and Son 2007). Two aspects of this definition are relevant here: (i) inclusive development creates opportunities across multiple dimensions—economic, social, cultural and political (Labonté, Hadi, and Kauffmann 2011); and (ii) it emphasizes processes and mechanisms rather than outcomes.

Inclusion can be viewed through the lens of its opposite—exclusion (World Bank 2013). Exclusion can occur at all income levels, but affects the poor most. Empirical studies typically find higher rates of poverty among excluded subgroups of the population—for example, minority religious or ethnic groups, indigenous peoples, the elderly, and women. Exclusion is often associated with identity—gender, age, religion, race, ethnicity, or place of origin. Identity-based exclusion can have deep historical roots. A legacy of oppression, wars and conflicts can create long-lasting social divisions, prejudices, and barriers.

Inclusion (and exclusion) emphasizes the following mechanisms and processes:

- access to adequate material resources and necessities, including adequate housing;
- having sufficient income—including state subsidies or transfers—to access adequate material resources and necessities, and to participate in the economy and society;
- access to labor markets and decent jobs (partly but not only to earn income);
- access to quality education and health care, including early childhood development;
- freedom from discrimination and victimization;

- freedom from excessive insecurity and danger, both economic and personal;
- having opportunities for social participation; and
- holding sufficient power or voice to influence government policy choices.

Key elements of an inclusive policy agenda for the PRC (and other upper-middle-income countries) should include: (i) promoting sustained, inclusive growth; (ii) continued investment in human capital and capabilities; (iii) addressing demographic change; and (iv) developing tailored, multidimensional interventions for excluded groups.

These areas provide a valuable template for policies that reduce vulnerability in the groups cited in this report.

Promoting Sustained, Inclusive Growth

Economic growth has slowed, with growth in 2018 the slowest in two decades. It is debatable whether this means the PRC will fall into the "middle-income trap"—whereby countries that have reached middle-income status experience slowing productivity and GDP growth (Glawe and Wagner 2017) (Figure 3). The government calls this a "new normal" and expects future growth to remain slower than in the past—even after the pandemic shock.

When growth slows, the trade-offs between policies and interest groups become more unpalatable, making policy choices more difficult.

Slowing growth creates problems for inclusive development. Rapid growth generates new opportunities for inclusion and gives governments leeway to redistribute the gains from growth. But when growth slows, the trade-offs between policies and between interest groups become increasingly stark, making policy choices more difficult. Thus, key components of the inclusive growth agenda are policies that sustain economic growth. These should focus on (i) increasing productivity (including via technological change), research and development, improving human capital, and reducing economic distortions and imbalances; (ii) investment in underlying productive infrastructure, such as transportation, power, communication and information technology; and

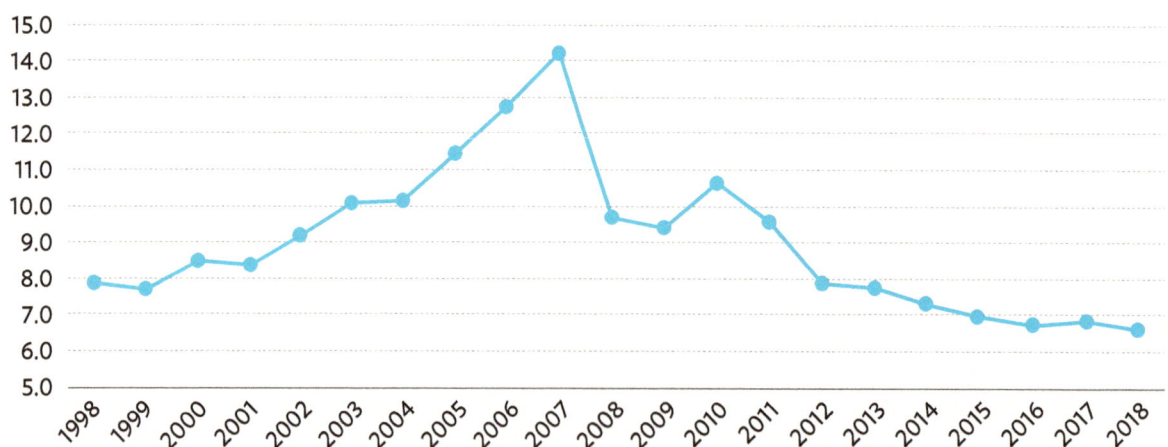

Figure 3: Gross Domestic Product Growth, 1998–2018
(%)

Note: In constant prices.
Source: National Bureau of Statistics http://www.stats.gov.cn/tjsj/ndsj/2018/indexeh.htm (accessed 31 August 2019).

(iii) improvements in institutional infrastructure, such as the legal and financial systems.

Continued Investment in Human Capital and Capabilities

Employment guarantees inclusivity but largely depends on individual skills—a reflection of enhanced human capital.

A key aspect of inclusive growth is expanding employment, ideally in the form of decent jobs and rising wages. Technology policies should thus prioritize change that generates employment. It is also important to promote higher value-added production and programs that help workers gain the skills required by new technologies.

In upper-middle income economies, employment requires higher knowledge and better skills. Those without these will lack the ability to participate fully in the evolving economy. An inclusive

development agenda therefore requires investing in education and training that satisfies the three-pronged policy of early childhood education, secondary and tertiary education, and lifelong learning and employment mobility.

Tackling Demographic Change

An aging society poses problems in labor supply and the availability of resources for social services.

The transition to middle- or upper-middle income status is often accompanied by demographic change. Rapid population growth early in the development process is followed by declining fertility (Figure 4).

In the PRC, the share of working-age population (20–64) peaked during 2015–2020. Projections show the shares of the young and working-age populations will decline and the share of the

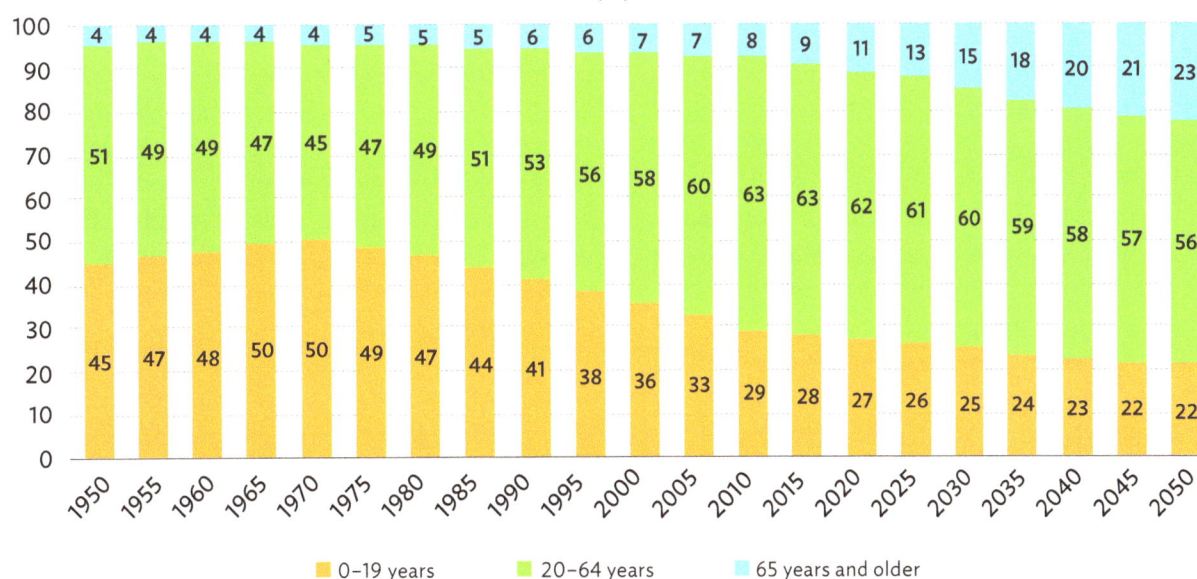

Figure 4: Past and Projected Composition of the Population by Age Group in Upper-Middle-Income Countries and the People's Republic of China
(%)

Legend: ■ 0–19 years   ■ 20–64 years   ■ 65 years and older

Source: United Nations, Department of Economic and Social Affairs, Population Division. 2019. World Population Prospects 2019, custom data acquired via https://population.un.org/wpp/DataQuery/.

elderly (65 and older) will rise. For the PRC, the share of the elderly is projected to rise to 17% by 2030 and 26% by 2050 (United Nations 2019). The ramifications of this aging have already been discussed.

Interventions for Excluded Groups

Many highly vulnerable groups are already marginalized by society.

As countries attain upper-middle and high-income status, certain groups are excluded and left behind. This is an extension of the analysis of vulnerable segments of the population. The factors causing exclusion can be complex, and often differ for various groups.

The groups excluded vary across countries, but are commonly related to several attributes: gender; identifiable minorities (ethnic, racial, religious); place of origin (migrants and immigrants); location (rural or remote regions); the elderly; and those with physical or mental disabilities.

(a) Gender. Women have made great strides in the PRC across many areas. Importantly, the gender gap in education has largely been eliminated. But barriers for women remain and, according to some studies, may have in increased in recent years (World Economic Forum 2018; Golley, Zhou, and Wang 2019; Qin 2019). Women face discrimination in hiring, promotion, and pay once they enter the workforce. This discrimination is exacerbated by retirement and pension policies, parental leave policies, child and elderly care access and the design of schooling, which have differential effects on women and men.

Outside work, women face barriers at home and in society. They face the risk of abuse and violence. Due in part to employment and legal disadvantages, women have less capacity to accumulate assets than men. Property rights and laws place women at a disadvantage with respect to housing ownership and rural land rights. Consequently, women are more vulnerable both socially and economically.

(b) Identifiable minorities. Not all minority groups feel excluded. But for some the degree of exclusion is high. For those that face exclusion, the nature of the exclusion is heterogeneous—for example, between those that live in areas where they are the majority versus those living interspersed among the majority, between rural versus urban settings, depending on language, religious and cultural factors, and as a result of different histories (for example, involving past conflict, exploitation, and land expropriation).

The exclusion of minorities is sometimes reinforced by government policy—for example, law enforcement (differential rates of incarceration); schooling; barriers to voter registration and political participation; and the absence of effective civil rights laws. Exclusion is a global phenomenon found in countries at all levels of development.

(c) The disabled. In most societies, the disabled are excluded in the sense that they cannot participate fully in society. Rates of poverty for the disabled are relatively high. Disability of a family member often affects the entire household. Consequently, poverty rates are also relatively high for households with a disabled member. Disability affects not only income, but costs of living, so households above the monetary poverty line can nevertheless be impoverished.

A range of policies promote inclusion of the disabled. These include financial support, caregiving support, and policies that improve access to education, employment, housing, and social and cultural participation, among others (UNDESA 2018, Chapter V). Effective policies to assist the disabled also require good statistics. To promote the development of a good database, the UN publishes a set of guidelines and manuals to guide national governments in collecting, compiling and disseminating disability statistics.

(d) Rural residents and migrants. The exclusion of rural residents and rural-urban migrants is not unique to the PRC. But due to the *hukou* system and related policies, it is more pronounced (see section IV).

In dealing with vulnerability, however, it is crucial that the government ensures it had adequate fiscal resources to address the issues, and better matching resource mobilization with expenditures.

3 STRENGTHENING THE FISCAL SYSTEM TO HELP REDUCE VULNERABILITY

The Role of Public Goods and Services

Measures that reduce vulnerability usually increase public goods and services; but these require greater fiscal resources.

The PRC's rapid economic growth between 1978 and 2020 is largely attributed to its gradual embrace of market forces. However, without the right regulatory environment, market pressures from unfair competition, externalities, asymmetric information, and lack of coordination, for example, can lead to market failure. Effective government intervention can help balance raw market forces with optimal social outcomes. The supply of public goods and services can help create the right balance.

There are several examples of public goods or government interventions that can help reduce poverty and vulnerability:

(i)   Promoting rural land rights can increase agricultural productivity.
(ii) Direct subsidies to grain farmers or for buying new seed varieties and agricultural machinery can boost farm income and reduce rural-urban income gaps.
(iii) Modern agricultural infrastructure for small-scale or water-saving irrigation, reservoir reinforcement, soil improvement, mechanization, and ecological protection can increase productivity. Later, government support for rural roads and transport, telecommunications, electricity and energy supply promotes better market access. And rural livelihoods can improve through government support to rural education, public health and medical care, and social safety nets.
(iv) The PRC's "No. 1 central document" for 2008 called for higher rural public service provisions in rural education, basic medical services, family planning, rural culture, transportation, and rural utilities. These are currently offered through three main social security nets: the social assistance system; a new rural cooperative medical care system; and a new rural social pension insurance system.
(v)   A rural minimum living security system offers targeted cash transfers to rural residents whose annual net per capita income falls below local minimum living security standards.
(vi) Institutional framework and policy measures in recent years were designed to improve the agricultural and rural environment. These include the protection and rehabilitation of agricultural land resources, regulations on the use of chemical fertilizers, pesticides and other chemicals, and the protection of agricultural water resources.
(vii) The government also provides policy and financial support for vulnerable groups (Box 1) and rural migrants (Appendix).

This chapter draws on the background papers prepared by Naoyuki Yoshino and Akiko Terada-Hagiwara, (Yoshino, Terada-Hagiwara, and Miyamoto 2021); Guoqin Zhao (2020a, 2020b); Guangdong Provincial Department of Finance, the PRC, 2021; and Hunan Provincial Department of Finance, the PRC, 2021.

Box 1: Vulnerability and Fiscal Sustainability at the Provincial Level

The provincial studies conducted and presented here address various aspects of the relationship between fiscal policy and vulnerability. The case study of Guangdong Province focuses on measures that can enhance the efficacy and efficiency of spending programs. The Hunan case study describes how spending programs are directed at specific vulnerable groups.

Guangdong Province

Guangdong's poverty reduction fully considers different situations in the eastern, western and northern parts of the province. Guangdong effectively prevents the poor population from falling back to poverty through financial investment, targeted measures, and co-investment from the private sector. On the one hand, Guangdong invests government financial resources into industrial development projects to further sustain public spending from the policy design angle; on the other hand, Guangdong tries to leverage social resources with financial funds to make joint efforts in poverty reduction with remarkable results achieved through such measures as establishing village-enterprise partnerships and Poverty Relief Day activities.

First, enhance financial investment with diversified support for poverty reduction.

1. *Allocate general purpose transfer payment to build the financial capacities of prefectures and counties to solve local social and economic issues, including poverty reduction.* In 2020, Guangdong transferred the general purpose payment totaling CNY177.8 billion to 86 counties (cities, districts) in the east, west, north areas and economically backward areas in the Pearl River Delta. This focused on key aspects such as balanced transfer payment from the provincial level to the above-mentioned counties (cities, districts), financial compensation for ecological protection zones, basic financial guarantee at the county level, subsidies for ethnic minority areas and underdeveloped former revolutionary bases;

2. *Improve precise fund investment in poverty reduction with funds used in prioritized areas.* Guangdong prioritizes poverty reduction efforts in the education sector, industrialization, employment assistance, health care sector and the population eligible for subsistence allowances, to promote the equalization of basic public services. These measures are elaborated as follows:
   (a) **Well targeted poverty reduction measures in the education sector:** in 2020, Guangdong invested CNY776 million to support 30,0000 students, ensuring that students would not be absent from school due to family economic difficulties;
   (b) **Strong policy support for employment and entrepreneurship:** Guangdong invested CNY25.5 billion of poverty alleviation and

development funds from 2016 to 2018 for industrialization and employment assistance to the poor households with working capacities; in 2020, Guangdong arranged CNY1.9 billion of special funds at the provincial level to support employment and entrepreneurship proposals and activities, including Cantonese Cuisine Master project, Guangdong Housekeeping project, e-commerce development in rural areas, guarantee loan discount and subsidy for start-ups;
   (c) **Coverage expansion of poverty reduction funds in the health care sector:** Guangdong allocated CNY3.3 billion for urban and rural medical aid at the provincial level in 2020, ensuring that over 80% of urban and rural low-income population and the poor population on file are covered with medical aid across the province, especially the underdeveloped areas;
   (d) **Targeted poverty alleviation for the population eligible for subsistence allowances:** Guangdong allocated CNY9.1 billion as relief fund for the poor and needy in 2020: the per capita compensation standards for urban and rural residents eligible for subsistence allowances in the province, especially in east, west and north Guangdong are CNY609 and CNY276, respectively; the basic living support for the extremely poor is no less than 1.6 times of the local minimum living level; the living of poor households unable to work is fully covered with policies;
   (e) **Poverty reduction upgrade through consumption:** From 2019 to 2020, Guangdong invested CNY44 million at the provincial level to support the construction of high-level poverty reduction cooperation trading markets for goods produced in underdeveloped areas across the country; built a total of 254 special trading markets, which attracted enterprises from 17 provinces in the central and western regions and those from 21 prefectures in Guangdong with over 8,500 kinds of products from 3,200 enterprises on exhibit for sale; identifies 962 "vegetable basket" production bases for the Greater Bay Area of Guangdong, Hong Kong, China and Macau, China in 19 provinces (autonomous regions and municipalities); and

3. *Deepen the reform of pooling agriculture related funds at the provincial level, and allow prefectures and counties to invest in urgent and mature projects with flexibility.* In 2020, Guangdong arranged CNY25.6 billion of agriculture related funds for prefectures and counties, which can use funds for poverty reduction and rural living environment improvement after completing performance targets assigned by the provincial government, so as to vigorously promote rural revitalization.

continued on next page

Box 1 *continued*

Second, fully leverage financial funds to direct social resources to poverty reduction.

1. ***Implement the tax relief policy and encourage enterprises and public institutions to actively participate in poverty reduction.*** The donation of poverty relief materials is exempted from value-added tax, and income tax of poverty relief donation is deducted pre-tax. Guangdong promotes tax-free policies for financial funds and administrative fees related to poverty relief and relocation projects, as well as other tax preferential policies to support entrepreneurship and employment;

2. ***Bring in the private sector to invest in poverty alleviation to broaden fund-raising channel.*** Since 2002, Guangdong has been promoting partnership between the Pearl River Delta area and the eastern, western and northern areas, with a total investment of CNY13.1 billion; has initiated village-enterprise partnership to deepen cooperation between paired villages and enterprises, with 9,115 enterprises investing CNY6.7 billion; has taken the lead in the PRC to organize the June 30 Poverty Relief Day activities for 10 years already, with more than 1,000 social organizations, almost 10,000 enterprises, over 1 million volunteers and 20 million caring people participating, and more than CNY32 billion of funds from the private sector accumulatively collected.

Third, strengthen poverty reduction with development projects to build endogenous growth capacities.

Guangdong not only reduces poverty through industrialization and employment assistance, but also explores a consumption-driven model to comprehensively empower the poverty-stricken areas.
Poverty reduction through industrialization: The provincial government, from 2018 to 2020, invested CNY7.5 billion to construct 150 provincial-level modern agricultural industrial parks in the eastern, western and northern parts of Guangdong; from 2019 to 2021, invested CNY1 billion annually to promote featured industries and products from villages and towns to increase income for the poor and reduce poverty.
Poverty reduction through employment assistance: Guangdong arranges special funds to build "poverty reduction base" and "poverty reduction workshop" to realize one-on-one contact between the poor and enterprises; strengthens the fund guarantee of vocational training projects with "Cantonese Cuisine Master" project delivering 12,000 training opportunities, and the "Guangdong Housekeeping" project completing 23,100 training opportunities. Poverty reduction through consumption: Guangdong builds an e-commerce platform for government purchase of goods from the underdeveloped areas to encourage consumption with government example.

Fourth, be forward-looking and link targeted poverty reduction with rural revitalization.

With new opportunities opened up by the policy to "prioritize the development of agriculture and rural areas", Guangdong explores the long-term mechanism to deal with relative poverty, and links poverty reduction and rural revitalization with specific policies, operations and measures. In recent years, Guangdong has invested CNY31.3 billion to incentivize 2,277 poor villages to take the lead in the construction of new rural demonstration sites, which further integrate local ecological, industrial, tourism, cultural and other resources to build rural revitalization highlight projects through policy and fund coordination, resource aggregation, project complementarity and systematic planning. For example, Yingde (county) invested CNY220 million to build Xiniu Town Rural Revitalization Demonstration to drive up the village collective revenue and villagers' incomes.

Fifth, comprehensively strengthen the supervision of poverty reduction funds to ensure transparency and safety.

Supervision, inspection and auditing of poverty reduction funds: Guangdong organizes inspections on the use of poverty reduction funds and simultaneously implements "dual monitoring" on the performance targets and allocation progress, so as to ensure accurate and efficient fund use.

Dynamic monitoring system of poverty reduction funds: Guangdong uses modern information technologies such as cloud computing and big data to build a simple, practical and real-time synchronous dynamic monitoring system, and realizes the dynamic monitoring of poverty reduction funds and projects. As of end December 2019, 42 central and 48 provincial funds totaling CNY131 billion are under the dynamic monitoring scope. Poverty reduction asset management system: Guangdong will further build a long-term and stable poverty reduction mechanism, enhance the achievements gained in various projects, build a solid material foundation to effectively link comprehensive poverty reduction with rural revitalization, and prevent the idleness, loss and waste of assets.

Hunan Province

The analysis for Hunan Province shows how the local government calibrates fiscal policy to address specific vulnerable groups—including the elderly living in poverty, people with disabilities, and migrant workers and their children.

To reduce poverty, Hunan provides subsidies to vulnerable groups, with most funding sourced from government financial investments. Subsistence allowances cover 2.2 million urban and rural residents,

continued on next page

Box 1 continued

with CNY40.7 billion allocated from 2014 to 2018. For the elderly who are poor, 135 home care information service platforms were built from 2012 to 2017. In 2018, 295,000 beds were available in senior care institutions; more than 4,000 urban community service centers for the elderly were built. In 2019, 4,736 people with disabilities were registered as poor, with plans for 20,000 disabled people to receive care in 2020. In addition, more than 3,000 left-behind children homes were built from 2014–2017. By 2020, they will be available in all administrative villages.

Hunan has continued to improve infrastructure to benefit vulnerable groups, including elderly service facilities, protection centers for minors, nursing institutions for the disabled, and children's homes in villages. Specific projects include a 3-year action plan (2020–2022) for improving the quality and upgrading special needy support institutions. These include construction of the "Elderly Service Safety Network" project at the county and city levels, a paired assistance project of nursing institutions for people with disabilities, and a provincial-level social welfare construction project for the elderly and children, among others. In 2019, the civil affairs department invested CNY24.6 million to construct social elderly service facilities. There are 22 regional nursing homes for the elderly, with 14 protection centers built for minors. "Children's Homes" will soon be available in all administrative villages. These have all strengthened the supply capacity and quality of public service facilities for the vulnerable.

For groups having difficulty paying pension insurance premiums, county and city governments cover the minimum standard. The province has realized its goal of "covering all the elderly people living in poverty with pension insurance." In 2018, Hunan Province paid CNY157 million in pension insurance for 1.7 million poor people, and directly granted CNY1.6 billion in old-age pensions for the elderly.

The province provides living allowances through its social assistance system directly to the elderly who are poor, people with disabilities, and left-behind children. Those 60-80 years old can enjoy a monthly living allowance of CNY50-100, with those over 80 a monthly living allowance of CNY100 or more. In 2020, the basic pension service subsidy has been fully covered; people with disabilities can enjoy a CNY60 monthly living allowance and CNY60 monthly nursing allowance; the allowance standards for centrally supported orphans and those living outside are CNY1,350/month and CNY950/month, respectively. From 2014–2017, people with disabilities received CNY1.3 billion in subsidies. In 2019, an average 21,000 orphans received living allowances monthly.

For children from impoverished families "facing difficulty in receiving education", the province spent CNY8.4 billion in various grants from 2014 to March 2020 covering 4.3 million students. It invested CNY9.0 billion to build "Furong Schools" for impoverished primary and secondary school students—100 "Furong Schools" are expected to be built by 2021, adding 146,900 compulsory education spots for students. In 2018, CNY3.6 billion was allocated by the central and provincial governments for training teachers working in rural areas and increasing their income.

To ensure the poverty-stricken population can access good basic medical services, Hunan uses a government assistance model for its poor. From 2014 to March 2020, it invested CNY8.5 billion on a "six-tier medical insurance" policy. The treatment rate for serious diseases in 51 poverty-stricken counties reached 99.3%; the contracted service rate for chronic diseases was reported to be 100%, with the comprehensive hospitalization reimbursement rate at 89.7%. In 2018, the actual reimbursement rate for the treatment of the poor in the province was 89.1%. Specific measures included the following:

1. *Improve medical infrastructure in poverty-stricken areas:* strengthen capacity building through standardizing county, township, and village level health services.

2. *Train grassroots medical staff in poverty-stricken areas:* supply free training of rural vocational medical students for free and assign them to health centers in poverty-stricken areas. The government also provides 3-year training for local publicly funded college prospects for grassroots medical and health institutions, and recruits 1,000 pre-assigned doctors to serve these areas each year—5,406 primary health workers were trained and recruited over the 5 years from 2014 to 2019. There is also a allowance system that subsidizes rural doctors working in these areas.

3. *Provide guarantees and subsidies for the poor to seek medical treatment:* the government uses a "one-stop" settlement and "payment after diagnosis and treatment" system to help the poor seek medical treatment—patients with chronic diseases receive contracted services from family doctors. Authorities have a financial subsidy policy that supplies the poor with the same basic medical insurance as urban and rural residents to receive medical assistance. In 2018, the provincial government allocated CNY1.6 billion in medical assistance funds. The province has a "free pre-marital medical check-ups" policy for residents in poor counties, and standardizes management of chronic diseases for people with disabilities and the elderly in poor areas.

Source: Wu, Jinhua, and Guangdong Provincial Department of Finance (2021) and Xiao, Haixiang, and Hunan Provincial Department of Finance (2021).

This all requires adequate fiscal resources. Estimates show a fiscal outlay of 7%-8% of GDP (from 9.4% in 2008) could bring aggregate "social expenditures" close to the lower end of high-income countries by 2030 (World Bank 2013). Recent trends in inclusive growth indicators—such as education, health, social security and employment—make this a difficult proposition. Projected increases in social spending will be 3%–4% of GDP below the 2030 threshold. In 2019, social fiscal spending was 8.2% of GDP, against the global average of 20.1% (UNESCAP 2019).

Fiscal Policy and Its Constraints

Financing public goods and services is increasingly challenging.

The demand for additional budgetary resources to address social and environmental needs comes at a time when PRC public spending is already high relative to GDP. Structural budget deficits could potentially erode available fiscal space and pose a risk to future fiscal stability. Thus, this report explores policies that improve the quality of life of vulnerable groups but do not necessarily require fiscal support. There might also be a need to change the composition of government expenditures to address evolving strategic priorities while maintaining fiscal sustainability. This will require fiscal discipline as well as budgetary procedures that allow resource reallocation over time from lower- to higher priority government programs. How the PRC deals with two key factors—its decentralized fiscal system, and its public finance management system—will be central to achieving these objectives.

Policymakers must consider the effects of population aging on the macro-economy and macroeconomic policy.

Factors that increased the vulnerability of certain groups have also affected the availability of fiscal resources. Several studies have established the link between population aging and macroeconomic performance (IMF 2019; Honda, and Miyamoto 2020) and between population aging and the effectiveness of macroeconomic policy (Yoshino and Miyamoto 2017; Honda and Miyamoto 2020). Macroeconomic performance has a direct impact on the availability of fiscal resources. Meanwhile, policymakers have to calibrate fiscal policy depending on how it will be affected by population aging.

The studies cited show quantitatively that economic growth is relatively low in countries with aging populations. This is a result of both lower labor input and lower productivity. The decline in potential growth then adversely affects private sector investment. Not surprisingly, the working-age population tends to decline in economies with aging populations. At the same time, labor force participation often rises. An overall decline in labor supply can lead to lower consumption expenditure. An aging population also leads to higher social security costs. Pension benefits to retirees are financed by taxes paid by workers and government bond issuance. Given a fixed amount of pension benefits per retiree, a decline in the proportion of workers increases their individual tax burden. Thus, population aging can also reduce a worker's consumption due to a negative wealth effect.

The level of public debt tends to be higher when the population ages. This is usually the result of increased fiscal spending related to social security. Higher public debt eventually crowds out public spending.

An aging population also reduces the effects of monetary policy on inflation and output. This is usually a result of a decline in labor supply. Normally, an expansionary monetary policy will lead to a drop in interest rates that will encourage both consumption and investment expenditure. But the impact on consumption will be lower in an economy with fewer workers. In the case of investment, lower interest rates will not have the same effect if potential economic growth is constrained by a decline in labor supply.

More recent studies show that fiscal policy is similarly affected. Honda and Miyamoto (2020) find that in economies with a lower share of aged population, a positive government spending shock increases output. In contrast, in economies with a higher share of aged population, a government spending shock does not have a statistically significant impact on output. Moreover, during a recession, the positive output effects in aging economies are weaker than those in non-aging economies, while during booms the negative output effect is long-lasting with population aging. Their analysis also suggests a few possible channels through which population aging weakens the output effects of fiscal policy. Specifically, they include: (i) Ricardian-type responses and (ii) lower growth in labor supply (likely leading to lower growth prospects).

Population aging would therefore call for larger fiscal stimulus to support aggregate demand during a recession and thus require larger fiscal space to allow a wider swing of the fiscal position without creating concerns over fiscal sustainability.

The combination of lower economic growth, investment, consumption, a higher public debt, and less effective macroeconomic policy will either reduce fiscal revenues or narrow fiscal space.

The reduction in fiscal space and fiscal policy efficacy has implications for the availability of resources to support vulnerable groups.

The allocation may remain the same but must cover a larger group. This implies that resources will be overextended (see section I). A worst-case scenario would be that available resources actually decline. Allocating more resources to preserve the same level and quality of service may not be compatible with maintaining fiscal sustainability. There would be three general options to maintain the same level and quality of service. One is to increase government expenditure to cope with additional spending requirements while simultaneously generating more revenue to avoid widening the fiscal deficit. The second is to improve the efficiency or productivity of the service-provider. And the third is to obtain resources from outside government, which generally means the private sector.

Other Areas Relating to Vulnerability and Fiscal Space

Uneven fiscal decentralization and urbanization also affect vulnerability and fiscal space.

Part of the problem is that local or subnational governments rely primarily on shared—and largely inadequate—revenues. The financing gap is estimated at 30% on average (Ahmad and van Rijn 2020). To reduce this gap, the PRC must address several fiscal challenges:

(i)   Current intergovernmental functional assignments for mitigating risks need to be re-examined along with better provision of local services;

(ii) Local governments must have their own reliable revenue resources, both to support their functions and as an anchor for borrowing and credit;

(iii) Local tax options should be evaluated, emphasizing piggyback taxes on national personal income or carbon taxes;

(iv) A variety of local government financing instruments—including municipal bonds and public–private partnerships—should be considered; and

(v)   Adequate monitoring and the prudent management of subnational liabilities can help develop accurate and timely balance sheets across all levels of government.

In addition, urbanization is largely associated with rural migration. The influx of rural migrants has led to additional demand for social services. Foremost is educational and nutritional support for children left behind. Migrants also require government support for housing, social insurance, and skills training (see Appendix and section IV).

Policy Recommendations

There are four ways the PRC can reform its fiscal system by 2030: (i) while containing expenditures as a share of GDP, shift their composition to meet new challenges, such as increasing public spending for social and environmental investment; (ii) improve the efficiency of revenue mobilization, for example, by changing revenue structures; (iii) reform intergovernmental fiscal relations by better aligning resource availability with expenditure responsibility at different levels of government; and (iv) strengthen the management of government finances and improve the efficiency of public expenditures. This report deals with the first and third aspects. The second allows additional resources to be allocated to public services, one of three options listed earlier (see section I.5)—a possible response to an increase in the size of a vulnerable group or a reduction in fiscal resources.

Employing the Elderly

Keeping old people working increases productivity and improves the efficiency of the pension system, easing the pressure on fiscal resources.

A necessary policy with aging populations is to keep older people working at the wage level of marginal labor productivity. In the long run, allowing the elderly to continue working will increase output and lead to a higher level of consumption. If the elderly remain healthy and continue working, they will not rely as much on social welfare, reducing both taxes required and the tax burden of the younger generation—which will see their disposable income and consumption rise.

In Asia, the lower income of the elderly is only partly because relatively few are employed (Terada-Hagiwara, et al. 2018). The major reason is lower productivity, and hence lower wages. Training and retraining older workers will not only benefit the workers themselves but also augment the quantity and quality of the workforce. Also, age-friendly cities with age-friendly infrastructure would help the elderly remain productive in the labor market.

Future efforts could focus on developing a unified pension system, including the national pooling arrangement announced by Xi Jinping on 18 October 2017. The proposed national pooling arrangement would enhance fiscal sustainability by (i) removing inefficiencies; (ii) introducing equalization measures; (iii) strengthening the National Social Security Fund's asset management (improving rates on investment); and (iv) introducing a more efficient and equitable way of collecting social security contributions.

Balancing Resource Availability with Expenditure Responsibility

Policies should be designed so resource availability matches expenditure responsibility across government levels.

To address this mismatch, the PRC launched a series of reforms to improve fiscal sustainability (Zhao 2020a):

(i) The central government should better monitor budget performance management to strengthen budget performance and make expenditures more efficient, the PRC now includes all budget funds when evaluating budget performance by correlating results with allocations.

(ii) The ratio of shared VAT receipts between the central and local governments was adjusted from 75:25 to 50:50; while the consumption tax—formally exclusively transferred to the central government, is now split. The consumption tax reform is not a simple proportional adjustment between central and local governments, but relies more on the "backward consumption tax collection link to steadily increase local revenue." More recently, a new policy reform is being discussed as a result of the pandemic. The central government may begin transferring funds directly to counties as "grassroots" governments, not through provinces and cities. News reports say the State Council discussed this in October 2020.

(iii) To better manage government debt, debt refinancing—which was strictly prohibited when the local government debt management system was launched in 2014—is now allowed (the first "refinance bond" was issued in 2018). In addition, local government debt quotas are being increased substantially, particularly via the issuance of "special" bonds.

Box 2: Potential Subnational Tax Design Options

(i) National tax policies and administration can be adapted to local government needs, particularly relative to possible "piggybacks" on personal income tax and carbon tax.

(ii) The piggybacks protect local government revenue assignments better than shared revenue—as the piggyback does not vary with central tax rate adjustments.

(iii) The piggybacks can also become the basis to access credit, and as the local government can adjust the marginal rate within a set band, can be used to underwrite municipal bonds.

(iv) At the local level, a simple recurrent property tax based on occupancy and size/location of the property, linked to local services, can provide own-source revenues for cities and replace land sales, and also provides an anchor for sustainable access to credit for local infrastructure.

Source: Ahmad and van Rijn (2020).

The tax system remains an important driver of structural change: first by directly affecting incentives for firms and households and—at the local government level—by financing basic services; and second, by better defining how to access credit for local infrastructure. Box 2 lists possible local tax reforms.

Demand for Local Bond Issuance

Many local governments are increasing the issuance of bonds to finance their needs.

While there is a transfer scheme between central and local governments to address the mismatch between resource availability and expenditure responsibility, a gap remains. To fill the void, many local governments are increasing bond issuance to finance their needs (Figure 5). Thus, ensuring local government fiscal sustainability is critical.

Demand for bonds from the central government comes both from domestic and foreign investors. But local bond market demand is limited to domestic investors. Thus, both the supply and demand for government bonds must be considered when analyzing fiscal sustainability. The transfer from the central government to local governments will temporarily delay a sharp deterioration of the budget deficit, but it is not a long-term fix. Both central and local governments must assess the amount of existing debt comparison with the interest rate sensitivity of demand for government bonds (Yoshino, Terada-Hagiwara, and Miyamoto 2021).

One of the key reasons the PRC was able to grow so rapidly in its early stage of modern development was its focus on keeping rural development in step with its industrial transformation. Today it requires reinforcement to avoid any widening inequality.

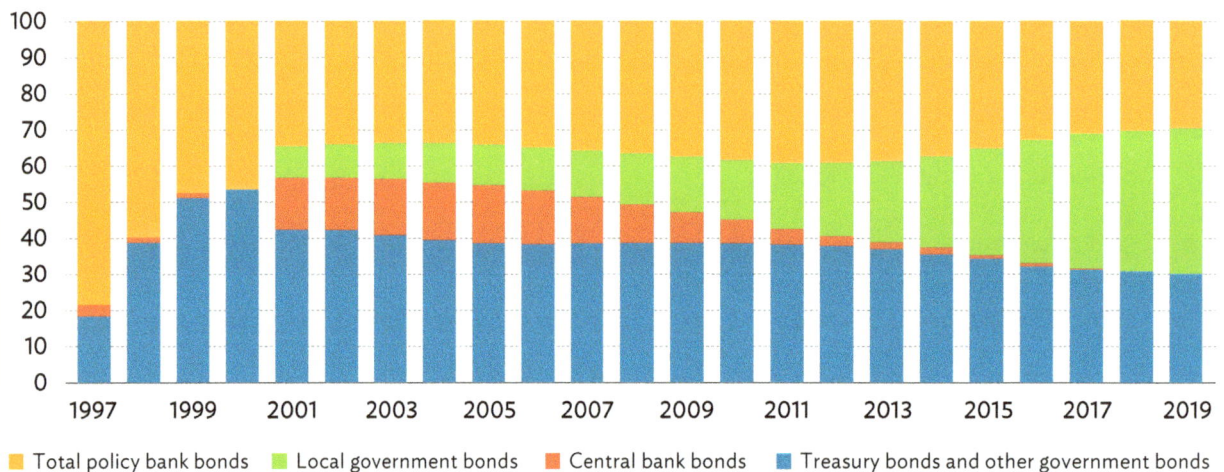

Figure 5: Composition of People's Republic of China Government Bonds, 1997–2019 (%)

Source: Yoshino, Terada-Hagiwara, and Miyamoto 2021.

REINVIGORATING SUSTAINABLE RURAL DEVELOPMENT

4

Poverty in Rural Areas

The PRC officially announced the eradication of absolute poverty in rural areas; but reducing relative poverty further and narrowing the rural-urban income disparity remain major policy issues.

Alleviating poverty in rural areas has been a top priority of the central government. From 1978 to 1985, the rural poor headcount fell from 250 million to 130 million (as measured by the PRC's 1978 poverty line of CNY200/person per year at 1984 prices.[3] During the mid-1980s, a planned process of poverty reduction and development was used to reduce regional imbalances, focusing on poverty alleviation in key poverty-prone areas. Using the 1978 poverty line, the poverty headcount dropped to 32.1 million and poverty rate decreased to 3.5% in 2000 (using the 2008 poverty line, the poverty headcount was 94.2 million and poverty rate 10.2% in 2000).

In the 2001–2010 decade, the poverty headcount decreased further to 26.9 million, or a poverty rate of 2.8% (based on the 2008 poverty line).

More recently—following the 18th Chinese Communist Party Congress in November 2012—a "targeted" poverty alleviation campaign resulted in a decrease in the rural poverty rate from 10.2% in 2012 to 0.6% in 2019.[4] The rural poor were heavily concentrated in the Western PRC,[5] where more than 55% of the poor resided (8.8% of the rural population in the Eastern Region was classified as poor). Provinces and even counties have undertaken these campaigns (Box 3).

A rural-urban poverty comparison is not straightforward. Some researchers (for example, Xia et al. 2007) argue that the national poverty line is too low to measure urban poverty—and thus underestimates the urban poor. Urban residents receiving the minimum living provision (*Dibao*) are frequently considered poor. During 2007–2017, the urban *Dibao* population decreased from 22.4 million to 12.6 million, with its share of the urban population dropping from 3.7% to 2.1%. In 2016, the average per capita income in urban areas was 2.7 times that in rural areas, indicating that the new poverty strategy should still promote rural development.

This chapter draws on the background papers prepared by Shingo Kimura, Wusheng Yu and Mingxi Han (Kimura, Yu, and Han 2021) and Provincial Poverty Reduction Case Research Group of Yunnan Provincial Department of Finance, the PRC, 2021.

---

[3] The poverty line in 1978 was CNY200/person per year at 1984 prices. By this measure, the PRC's rural poverty rate was 30.7% in 1978 and 14.8% in 1985. Since then, the poverty line has been revised twice.

[4] See Government Work Report (Onsite Record)—22 May 2020, at the Third Session of the Thirteenth National People's Congress, http://www.cpad.gov.cn/art/2020/5/22/art_61_123261.html.

[5] The Eastern Region comprises 11 provinces, including Beijing, Tianjin, Hebei, Liaoning, Shanghai, Jiangsu, Zhejiang, Fujian, Shandong, Guangdong, and Hainan; Central Region comprises 8 provinces, including Shanxi, Jilin, Heilongjiang, Anhui, Jiangxi, Henan, Hubei, and Hunan; Western Region comprises 12 provinces, including Inner Mongolia Autonomous Region, Guangxi Zhuang Autonomous Region, Chongqing, Sichuan, Guizhou, Yunnan, Tibet Autonomous Region, Shaanxi, Gansu, Qinghai, Ningxia Hui Autonomous Region, and Xinjiang Uygur Autonomous Region.

Box 3: The Case Study of Yongsheng County in Yunnan Province

The recent experience of Yongsheng County, Yunnan Province, describes the general measures taken to improve efficacy and efficiency as well as specific programs that address poverty and vulnerability.

Yongsheng County covers northwestern Yunnan and central Lijiang, a 4,950 square kilometer area with a population of 406,800, three-quarters of which live in rural areas. Ten ethnic minorities account for 140,000 people, or 34.4% of the population. They include the Yi, Lisu, Tibet, and Pumi ethnic minorities, among others. The county has registered 16,211 households with 62,215 people as poor, mostly ethnic Lisu.

In the 5 years from 2014 to 2019, 15,117 households with 58,912 people were officially lifted out of poverty—equivalent to 94 villages. The poverty incidence rate dropped from 18.0% to less than 1.0%. Three measures were behind this dramatic drop:

1. *Coordinate and integrate funds to strengthen financial security:* to ensure the war against poverty would succeed, authorities used all resources available to provide financial guarantees for the fight against poverty. The proceeds from the country's capital investments rose annually, while other expenditures were kept to a minimum. Since 2016, CNY266.5 million was added to the county's revenue. Another measure has been to coordinate and integrate financial agriculture-based and special poverty alleviation funds were also used. Authorities prioritized allocating funds, projects, and personnel to poor areas. "two assurances, three guarantees."[a] Coordinated financial management and the active participation of all stakeholders helped.

2. *"Six grasps and six determinations" to strengthen poverty alleviation fund management:* since 2018, with help from the specially assigned Ministry of Finance poverty alleviation work team, Yongsheng County adopted the "six grasps and six determinations"[b] concept in managing poverty alleviation funds. The system applies rules that focus on where and how funds are used and monitoring to identify problems. The management and institutional structure of how funds are used is tightly controlled. A "horizontal to side, vertical to bottom"[c] framework ensures all are covered. Since 2018, Yongsheng County's fund management for poverty alleviation has consistently ranked among the best among People's Republic of China provinces and cities.

3. *Precise monitoring to ensure poverty alleviation is effective:* only by setting the right "prescription" can the "poor roots" be pulled out. Authorities used a "Ten Major Projects" approach to ensure poverty alleviation measures were effective. The projects cover an array of economic and social sectors:

(a) **Industry.** CNY1.0 billion of budget funds and CNY573 million in poverty alleviation loans were issued, with a "reward for subsidy" approach adopted to help develop 84 specific industries— including high-quality beef cattle.

(b) **Employment.** A total of 64,964 poor laborers were trained, with each household involved with more than one skill; 22,878 poor laborers changed jobs, covering 1.4 people per household.

(c) **Relocation.** CNY152 million was invested to build 12 centralized relocation sites (including one decentralized relocation area) to relocate 757 households with 2,857 people.

(d) **Education.** CNY399 million went to 317 school construction projects, 41 new kindergartens, 2,272 sets of teaching equipment and living facilities, and to cover rural teacher living subsidies.

(e) **Ecology.** Authorities selected 4,466 poor people registered to become ecological forest rangers and paid CNY74.6 million in wages, benefiting 74,373 poor households.

(f) **Health.** Authorities invested CNY24.1 million to build 136 village clinics, equipped with 412 practicing registered village doctors; to cover 100% of the basic medical insurance, critical illness insurance and medical assistance system for the poor.

(g) **Safety net.** Among the county's registered poor, 9,167 households with 15,386 people enjoy the minimum living allowance.

(h) **Housing.** Since 2014, CNY756 million was invested to renovate 41,505 households, or 44.3% of the county total, to renovate dilapidated, thatched houses, and other houses to ensure they were safe.

(i) **Drinking water.** The water conservancy project invested CNY948 million on several water conservation projects, assuring safe drinking water, efficient use of water resources in Longkaikou and the Xiaomi Tian Reservoir.

(j) **Basic upgrading.** Infrastructure investments boosted access to convenient transportation, electricity, network broadband, radio and television; it helped create a village collective economy to strengthen its grassroots.

---

[a]   Refers to assuring that the rural poor population will have enough food and clothing and guaranteeing that they have access to compulsory education, basic medical services and safe housing (Guangdong case study).

[b]   "six grasps" refer to: (i) establishment of the poverty alleviation fund system including targets, (ii) set rules for the management of poverty alleviation funds, (iii) focus on the core goal of "where the poverty alleviation funds are used, (iv) where the system is followed up, (v) where the problems are, and (vi) where is the system perfect."

[c]   Means full coverage.

Approach to Rural Development

The PRC's rural development policies have been consistently effective; strategic adjustments have been made over time, with now an appropriate time to do so again.

The country has placed agriculture, farmers, and rural areas (the three *nong*) at the core of its policy agenda to become a moderately prosperous society (*xiao kang*). It successfully adjusted rural development strategies to fit the rapidly evolving socio-economic situation (Table 2). Initial policy reforms in the late 1970s focused on boosting food production and maintaining grain self-sufficiency. The policy evolved in the mid-1990s to increase competitiveness through agricultural modernization and economic diversification. Since the 2010s, rural policy has become more integrated and balanced to improve the economic, social and environmental welfare in rural areas. Support to agriculture also gradually shifted from maintaining grain self-sufficiency to ensuring long-term food security through sustainable use of natural resources.

Agricultural reform and poverty reduction anchor the rural development strategy.

The overall rural development strategy has always revolved around agricultural production and rural poverty. These two are closely linked to landownership and land use. In the economic reform and "opening up" era, the PRC leadership (the Central Committee of the Communist Party of China [CCCPC] and State Council) released a series of agricultural and rural development documents ("No. 1 central documents") outlining major policy priorities and measures.

Rural Land Rights Reform and Land Market Development

Rural reforms centered on land rights, which allowed for the establishment of the household responsibility system.

Land rights have always been at the core of rural reforms. Since the founding of the PRC, four rounds of major land reforms have been carried out, initially transitioning from individual

Table 2: Evolution of Agriculture and Rural Development Policy

Period	Late 1970s–Mid 1990s	Late 1990s to late 2000s	2010–Present
Objectives	Increase food production and grain self-sufficiency	Increase farm income; Agricultural competitiveness; Product quality and safety	Sustainable development of agriculture; Improving rural economic, social and environmental welfare; Targeted poverty reduction for a moderately prosperous rural society
Instruments	Household responsibility system—separating collective landownership and individual land use rights; Marketing and procurement reforms for grains and other crops; Investment in basic infrastructure; Land tax	World Trade Organization accession and agriculture trade policy reform; Abolishment of agricultural taxes; Introduction of price based and direct subsidies to boost production; Incentives for agricultural mechanization and other measures to modernize agriculture	Moderate food import; Investment in research and development; Increased provision of basic services and public goods; Partner with other industries, such as information and communication technology; Investment in rural environmental infrastructure; Rural vitalization and integrated urban-rural development strategy

Source: Asian Development Bank.

ownership to collective ownership, then to the household responsibility system under collective ownership, which distinguishes land use rights from landownership (Zheng, Luo, and Hong 2019).

The 1950s Land Reform Law abolished "feudal land ownership and implementation of peasant land ownership", allowing peasants the right to own, use, transfer and benefit from their allocated land. In 1956, the Model Charter of Agricultural Production Cooperatives started **collective landownership by villages** (NPC 1956). Individual farmers eventually joined "production teams" with agricultural production farmed on collectively owned land. This system significantly reduced individual farmer incentives and slowed agricultural development.

After the Cultural Revolution ended in 1976, the **household responsibility system** was established, which returned operating rights over land to individual farm households, while villages continued to own land collectively. The first five "No.1 central documents" issued during this period provided the basic policy framework for these initial agricultural and rural reforms.[6] It ignited rapid agricultural production growth as they allowed farmers to make their own production decisions. This enabled the country to secure grain security.

The fourth major change in land institution reform was promulgated in 2014, when the CCCPC and State Council issued its *"Opinions on guiding the orderly transfer of rural land management rights and developing moderate scale agricultural management"*. It stressed the need to "adhere the collective ownership of rural land, stabilize farmers' contracting rights, and 'loosen up' land management rights". It created a *"**three rights**

separation" of (i) ownership, (ii) contractual rights, and (iii) management rights among villages, farmers, and farm operators. Land contracts allowed the use of contracted land as a marketable asset that could generate dividends. They could also be used as collateral to obtain loans and credit.

This promoted a "clarification" of land contracts nationwide, based on the size and location of the contracted land. The certification strengthened the legal standing of land contracts and eliminated uncertainties associated with reallocating land at the village level (Li 2020). In practice, the certificates were produced by provincial governments and issued by county level governments under supervision of the Ministry of Agriculture. By the end of 2019, the "clarification" process covered 550,000 villages in 2,838 counties, with contracts covering 100 million hectares. With the increased security of land contracts and the government's blessing, land transfers increased dramatically through subcontracting, leasing, and shareholding, among others. This led to large-scale agricultural operations.

Urban areas are state-owned. With rapid urbanization, demand for land has increased with urban expansion, requiring additional supply of land from rural areas. However, converting collectively owned rural land into urban land is an onerous administrative process. For a long time, the conversion of arable land, rural construction land, and rural housing plots had been strictly controlled. Compounding this is the fact that rural residents normally cannot gain *hukou* rights in urban areas, nor can they be adequately compensated for converting land owned collectively. This has led to further pilot institutional reforms covering urbanization and the *hukou* system.

---

6   The No. 1 Central Document is the most important policy document in the PRC, jointly issued by the Central Committee of the Communist Party of China (CCCPC) and the State Council. This document, issued annually at the beginning of the year during 1982–1989 and again during 2004–2020, determines the most important issues and focus of the year. Agricultural and rural reforms were the focus of the No.1. Central Documents during 1982–1986. The issues related to agriculture, farmers, and rural area (the "Three *Nongs*") have again been the topic of this document since 2004.

Modern Agriculture to Spur Rural Growth

Innovative institutions support agricultural modernization to achieve economies of scale.

Professional farmer cooperatives emerge

In the late 1970s and early 1980s, rural households generally became the basic unit for agricultural production and management. This resulted in many individual farmers having to access the markets individually. This naturally demanded ways for farmers to better access markets. It led to the emergence of farmer professional technology associations and rural cooperative foundations that offered farmers more organized access to inputs and technology, as well as markets to sell produce. This in turn led to the further development of professional cooperatives in the 1990s, including technical/research associations, cooperatives, consortia, and service companies, among others.

The Law on Farmer Professional Cooperatives (FPCs) was promulgated and implemented in 2007. At least 80% of farmer professional cooperative members must be farmers, with each having one vote. By the end of 2019, there were 2.2 million legally registered farmer professional cooperatives (Figure 6). As a voluntary organization organized by agricultural producers, FPCs effectively boost farmer income and agricultural production, playing an important role in poverty alleviation and rural revitalization.

Support for farm incentives and income: tax reforms and direct subsidies

The "opening up" era saw a series of major reforms and economic adjustments. For much of this period, the CCCPC and State Council issued a series of agricultural and rural development "No. 1 central documents", outlining major policy priorities and measures, which basically set out the overall rural development strategies covering the last 4 decades. After the initial success of rural reforms—and the focus of economic reform shifted to urban areas—the PRC leadership stopped releasing annual No. 1 central documents, until 2004, when agriculture and rural development were again elevated to the top of policymaking processes. The 2004 No. 1 central document explicitly discusses increasing farm incomes and reducing rural-urban income gaps— applying direct subsidies to grain farmers and subsidies to purchase new seed varieties and agricultural machinery. The subsidies also aimed to increase agricultural production incentives and to

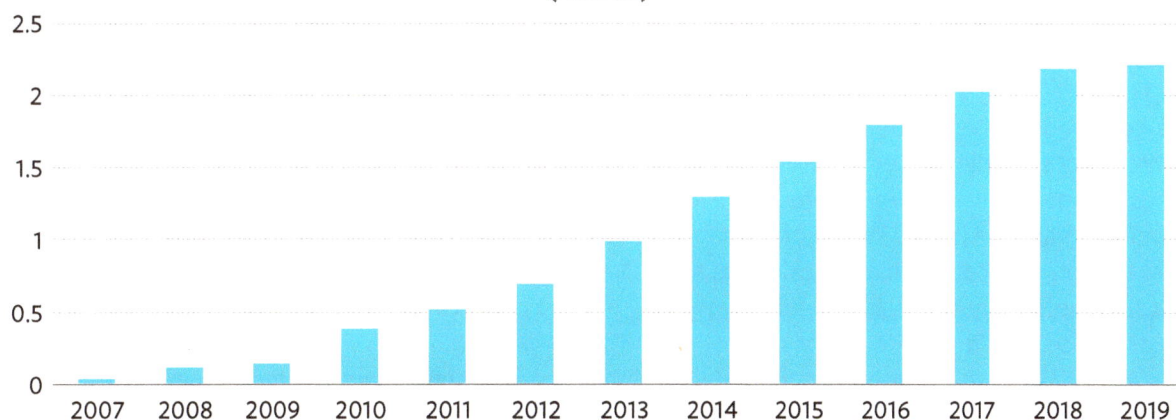

Figure 6: Professional Farmer Cooperatives
(million)

Source: State Administration for Industry and Commerce.

further reduce agricultural taxes. The 2005 No. 1 central document proposed additional measures to raise the "comprehensive production capacity" through strengthened agricultural support policies, particularly in the main grain producing provinces. The 2006 No. 1 central document used the theme "constructing socialist new rural area" to continue the emphasis on reducing taxes on agriculture and farmers and committed to increase transfer payments in agricultural and rural areas. Agricultural taxes historically based on annual agricultural output was formally ended.

Since the early 2000s, the Chinese government quickly shifted from applying agricultural taxes on farmers to broader support measures such as tariffs, tariff-rate quotas and various domestic subsidy programs. The agricultural support policy evolved quickly from ensuring 95% grain self-sufficiency to wider socioeconomic objectives—including environmental conservation. The support was gradually decoupled from commodity production; however, the costs associated with public stockholdings still comprise the major part of the agricultural expenditures. Shifting resources toward more forward-looking investments will help sustain agricultural growth.

The 2008–2009 global financial crisis and, more specifically, the ensuing hike in world food prices led the PRC to once again emphasize the need to ensure stable agricultural development and a secure domestic grain supply. The 2009 No. 1 central document thus set large increases in agricultural subsidies. The minimum purchase price for grains was increased in some main producing areas, and public stocks of food grains, cotton, vegetable oil, and pork were also raised. It should be noted that the minimum purchase price system for food grains—an important market price support program—was strengthened over the next several years.

Invest in modern agricultural infrastructure and production systems

Strong investment in network infrastructure facilitated rural industrialization.

The concept of "modern agriculture" became the central theme for agricultural and rural development in the No. 1 central documents from 2007 onwards. The focus was on agricultural and rural infrastructure (the No. 1 central documents in 2007, 2008, 2009, 2011); creating modern agricultural organizations such as cooperatives (2007 No. 1 central document); agricultural technology and innovation (2012 No. 1 central document); and institutional reforms in agricultural operations (2013 No. 1 central document).

The 2007 No. 1 central document integrates the concept of "modern agricultural development" into the overall "scientific development strategy". A modern agriculture system is built upon modern physical infrastructure, science and technology, production systems and operation methods—thus creating a new type of farmer. Finance for public investment in infrastructure and research and development, multi-functional agriculture and rural industries, market system development, and upgrading the rural labor force are key drivers of agricultural modernization.

Based on this, the 2008 No. 1 central document focused on *agricultural infrastructure*, including small-scale irrigation facilities, water saving irrigation, reservoir reinforcement, soil improvement, mechanization, and ecological protection projects. Water conservation was the focus of the 2011 No. 1 central document. Weak system links had to be strengthened, including irrigation facilities for arable land, small reservoirs, water shortages, flood and drought preparedness, and clean drinking water supply in rural areas.

The 2012 No. 1 central document addressed *agricultural research and innovation* to sustain agriculture supply—as intensive chemical fertilizer and pesticide use were unlikely to boost yields further. Therefore, further growth should come through productivity gains in land, resources, and labor.

Cultivating *new agricultural production and operation organizations* was the focus of the 2013 No. 1 central document. It dealt with organizing agricultural production and business operations, for example, through "family farms" and agricultural cooperatives; it said that a new mechanism designed to promote socialized agricultural services would allow service providers to thrive.

In terms of mechanization, the 2004 Agricultural Mechanization Promotion Law supported development of agricultural machinery social services (NPC 2004). Generally, two types of mechanization services exist in the PRC. One is mechanical services provided by "Specialized Custom Plowers, Planters and Harvester" teams, who own and operate large machines for smallholder plowing and harvesting needs. The other is machine rental markets, where households operate rented machines. The rapid mechanization in agriculture through professional service provision (also known as "socialized service provision") is an important institutional innovation. It allows farmers to access mechanized services when needed. Using these services rather than purchasing their own machines avoids unnecessary costs and increases efficiency (Guo, Liu, and Chen 2020).

Modernized agriculture allowed farmers more time to earn more income. Off-farm work now accounts for more than 70% of rural household income, as opposed to 25.6% in 1990.

Expanding Basic Rural Services and Safety Nets

Vulnerability to poverty has been reduced among rural households due to greater access to basic rural services and more effective social safety nets.

Through a series of No. 1 central documents (2007, 2008, 2015, and 2019), the provision of basic rural services and public goods, establishment of rural social safety nets, and rural governance have grown in importance to PRC rural development strategies. For instance, the 2008 No. 1 central document calls for increased rural public service provision, including education, basic medical services, family planning, rural culture, transportation, and utilities. The 2015 No. 1 central document describes equalized public service provisions as part of a "new rural area" campaign—covering rural education, medical care, culture, minimum living security, and rural pension insurance. This document also opens the door for private capital to participate in rural infrastructure and certain rural service provisions. The 2019 No. 1 central document again lists a series of areas where public service provisions will be strengthened—ranging from rehabilitating the rural housing environment, education, medical care, social security, pensions, and culture and sports. It emphasized "equalizing" basic service provisions between urban and rural areas.

The provision of rural public services is driven by three main social security safety net systems: the social assistance system, a new rural cooperative medical care system, and a new rural social pension insurance system. The goal is to expand and improve rural public service provision with a focus on basic universal medical care, care for the elderly and assistance to lower income residents (Cui 2020).

The rural minimum living security system

Since the mid-1990s, a rural minimum living security system has been in place. In 2007, the CCCPC and State Council issued a *"Notice on the Establishment of a Rural Minimum Living Security System in the Country"*, a social security system providing targeted cash transfers to rural residents with annual net per capita income below the local minimum living security standard. Initially, the threshold for receiving transfers was CNY840, lower than the CNY1,196 national poverty line—in 2015, it was raised above the national poverty line. Targeted recipients are mainly rural residents living with perennial difficulties such as sickness, old age, frailty, incapacity, or poor living conditions. In 2007, the system provided cash transfers to 16.1 million households across the country, or 35.7 million people. In 2017, coverage expanded to 22.5 million households and 40.5 million rural residents, or 7% of the total rural population (MCA 2017). In 2019, the program budget amounted to CNY112.7 billion (MCA 2019).

Medical Insurance System for Urban and Rural Residents

Beginning the second half of 2003, various regions launched pilot projects to establish a new rural cooperative medical care system—funded jointly by the central government, local government and farmers. The new system provides coverage for serious/critical illnesses that require hospitalization. In 2007, 85.5% of counties across the country adopted the new rural cooperative medical system, with 730 million farmers participating, a participation rate of 83% (Cui 2020). In 2016, the State Council integrated the new rural cooperative medical care system with the existing basic medical insurance for urban residents into a basic medical insurance for urban and rural residents, promoting the overall medical insurance for rural residents. As of end of 2020, there were more than 1.0 billion participants, plus 0.3 billion office employees, for a total of more than 1.3 billion people, or over 95% coverage of the total population. The per capita government medical expense reached CNY550, steadily improving the level of security.

The new rural social pension insurance system

In 2009, the rural pension insurance system began a pilot project for "new rural social pension insurance", backed by the combined funding of "individual contributions, collective aid, and government subsidies." Operated by the government, it aims to protect basic living conditions of elderly rural residents. Those with rural *hukou* aged 16 and above not participating in urban pension insurance are eligible for voluntary enrollment. Rural residents aged 60 and above can receive pension payments without paying fees, whereas those under 60 pay to join the scheme.

Investment in basic infrastructure

Investment in basic rural infrastructure was included in several No.1 central documents issued by the CCCPC and State Council. Initially, rural infrastructure was narrowly defined as agricultural infrastructure, mainly in the areas of arable land, agricultural irrigation, and more generally water conservancy. Its focus was expanded during the reform and opening up era to more diversified rural economic activities—such as roads and transport, telecommunications, electricity and energy supply, as well as infrastructure that improves rural livelihoods such as rural education, public health and medical care, and social safety nets.

The PRC also increased spending on rural basic infrastructure, resulting in significantly upgraded rural water supply, electricity and gas distribution, roads, and housing. This was part of the overall strategy to construct "beautiful and livable rural areas". According to the Third National Agricultural Census, by the end of 2016, 99.3% of all administrative villages nationwide could access public roads. By the end of August, 2020, all towns and administrative villages that meet the requirements will be open to passenger cars across the country. The share of villages with electricity reached 99.7% in 2016. The proportion of villages with cable television installed was 82.8% in 2016. In addition, nearly 90% of the villages across the country have internet connections. The increased access to information and communication technology (ICT) has given farmers the opportunity to conduct e-commerce. In 2016, about 25% of the villages across the country had e-commerce distribution sites, allowing farmers to sell via major e-commerce platforms and also to buy products for collection. The proliferation of e-commerce in some villages led to many villagers taking part in e-commerce activities, earning these villages the nickname "Taobao Villages".

Domestic living conditions in rural areas also improved and have been accelerating. In 2018, the per capita housing area for rural residents was 47.3 square meters, with 71.2% living in reinforced concrete houses or brick-concrete houses. Sanitary toilets were promoted, and sanitary facilities were improved and/or upgraded. Improved drinking water supply is available to more than 90% of rural residents. Through efforts from 2006 to 2020, the safety of drinking water for rural residents has been guaranteed. Clean water is available to rural residents instead of blackish water. Consumer durables for rural households have increased steadily, with significantly better quality and functionality. In 2016, for every 100 rural households, 89.5 owned refrigerators, 84.0 had washing machines and 118.8 color televisions—nearing the levels of their urban counterparts. Ownership of non-traditional durable goods also increased.

In addition, private capital has widely participated in rural infrastructure investment through the PPP model, effectively filling the gap in the development of public services that are badly needed in rural areas. During the 13th Five-Year Plan period, there were 379 PPP projects in agriculture and rural areas, covering 13 sectors such as transportation, education and health care. For example, the Jiangxi Smart Agriculture PPP project establishes a provincial unified smart platform to manage the whole process of agricultural production in a digitalized manner. It launches the 'Gannongbao' e-commerce platform to help match trade between villagers from remote and mountainous areas and the market, and promote agricultural products for free, with average monthly sales exceeding

CNY5 million. Another example is the PPP project for the comprehensive development of urban and rural education in Yucheng City, Shandong Province, which completed the renovation and expansion of 10 township schools and 4 city schools totaling 170,000 square meters in 1 year with a preliminary investment of CNY36 million and total investment of CNY340 million. The project has solved the renovation problem that had plagued the city for 20 years at one go and improved the overall educational and teaching conditions of 30,000 urban and rural students. Rural children can enjoy the best teaching environment without moving to cities.

Integrating Urban-Rural Development; Building a Moderately Prosperous Rural Society

A holistic approach to rural development will allow rural households to benefit from urban growth spillovers.

A recurrent theme of the PRC's rural development strategy is to reduce the apparent and persistent rural-urban income gap. The ratio of per capita disposal income of urban residents to rural residents was greater than 3 during 2003–2010, before dropping in 2010–2014 (Figure 7). The ratio has declined to 2.6:1 more recently. The income gap remains quite large, especially when compared with high-income countries. While rural poverty has been falling, the policy priority since 2015 has been targeted reductions on the remaining poor. This is an important component of the new poverty strategy.

In the most recent 2020 No. 1 central document, targeted poverty reduction is a precursor to a "moderately prosperous" society. In particular, remaining concentrations of poor households were prioritized. Another policy priority is to design long-term mechanisms to detect and prevent any return to poverty—in line with the emphasis on reducing vulnerability.

Figure 7: Annual Disposable Income of Urban and Rural Residents

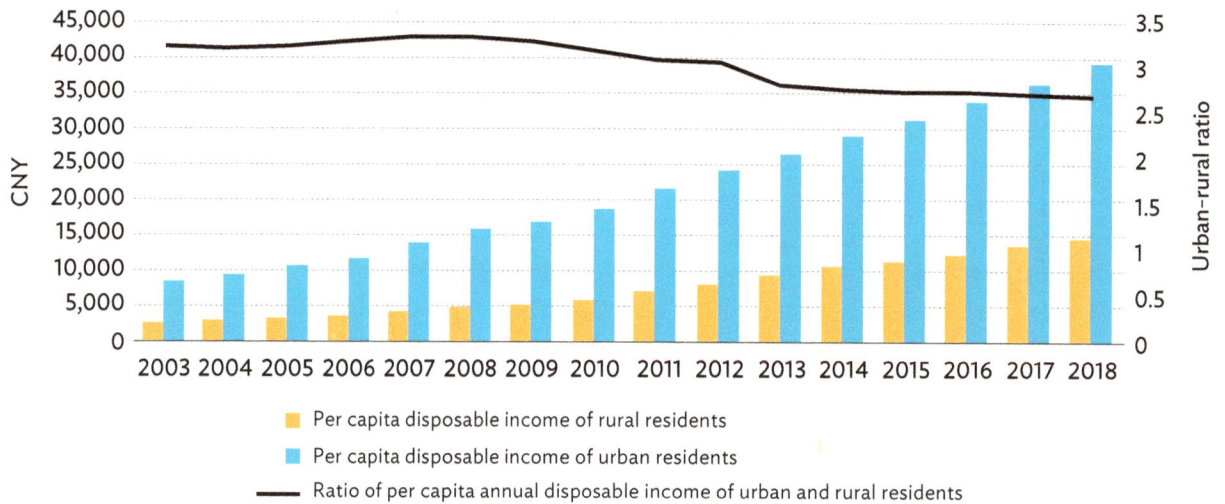

Legend:
- Per capita disposable income of rural residents
- Per capita disposable income of urban residents
- Ratio of per capita annual disposable income of urban and rural residents

Source: China Statistical Yearbook.

Rural vitalization and integrated rural-urban development

Excessive domestic production and high grain stocks has led to "agricultural supply-side reform", including agricultural structural adjustments and a changing focus on food safety and quality. This is in conjunction with "rural vitalization" and "integrated urban and rural development" strategies, as mentioned in several No. 1 central documents (2010, 2015, 2016, 2017). These also cover areas such as wider use of ICT in agriculture, green agriculture, and environmental protection.

The rural vitalization strategy was first proposed in Xi Jinping's report to the 19th CPC National Congress in October 2017 (Box 4).[7] The report labels agriculture, rural areas, and farmers as fundamental national issues with finding solutions key issues for the CPC. Following the 18th CPC National Congress, the Rural Vitalization Strategic Plan was formally announced by the CCCPC and State Council as "a major historic task for securing

a decisive victory in building a moderately prosperous society in all respects and for fully building a modern socialist country."

The plan outlines key tasks covering 2018–2022 toward meeting the strategy's overall goal of building rural areas with thriving businesses, a pleasant living environment, social etiquette and civility, effective governance, and prosperity.

An integrated urban-rural development approach ultimately requires *hukou* system reform.

The PRC has gradually shifted toward more integrated development connecting rural and urban areas. Economic activities in rural areas have diversified from primary agricultural production to processing and services. Rural tourism development also helped expand the economic linkage between rural and urban areas. Integrated development also implies more equitable public services provision, increasing

---

7   Source: http://cpc.people.com.cn/n1/2017/1028/c64094-29613660.html.

Box 4: Definitions of Rural Vitalization

Attaining a "moderately prosperous society" (MPS) is one of the main goals of the Rural Vitalization Strategy. The MPS concept was first proposed by Deng Xiaoping in 1979, with the initial goal reaching an average per capita gross domestic product (GDP) of $800 by the end of the 20th century. Since then, specific MPS indicators have been expanded and updated many times.

The Rural Vitalization Strategic Plan (CCCPC and State Council 2018) formally defines rural vitalization using five dimensions:

(i)   Thriving businesses: "solid" comprehensive agricultural production capacity, a high-quality agricultural supply system, integrated development of primary, secondary, and tertiary sectors in rural areas.

(ii) A pleasant living environment: adequate infrastructure, improved living environment, rehabilitated ecological environment, and equalization of basic public service provisions across urban and rural areas.

(iii) Rural civilization: high degree of civilization, good spiritual wellbeing, civilized rural social interactions, good family relationships, high morality.

(iv) Effective governance: party leadership, responsible government, social collaboration, public participation, and guaranteed rule of law, ensuring the rural society of vitality, harmony, and order.

(v)   Prosperous life: high quality employment, diversified income sources, reduced rural-urban income gaps.

For each dimension, specific goals and targets are set for a multitude of indicators for 2020 and 2022, using 2016 as base year. For example, in relation to the "prosperous life" dimension, specific targets during the 2016–2022 period are set regarding rural Engel coefficient (a reduction from 32.2% to 29.2%), urban-rural income ratios (decreasing from 2.7 to 2.6), penetration ratio of tap water (increasing from 79% to 85%), and qualified administrative villages connectivity to hard-surface roads (increasing from 96.7% to 100%). Similarly, targets such as livestock waste treatment, village green space, domestic waste treatment, modern toilets are set for the "pleasant living environment" dimension.

rural residents' access. In addition, the *hukou* household registration system and its attached social security system have also evolved over time, an important institutional framework determining the rural and urban linkage.

The guiding principle of integrated rural and urban development was included in the political report at the 19th National Congress of the CPC. The aim is to allow production factors to freely flow between urban and rural areas: in the transfer of capital, knowledge, information and entrepreneurship, and the free movement of rural labor and land to urban areas. Markets will play the decisive role in allocating these different factors. These guiding principles were further expanded in a CCCPC and State Council policy document, "*Opinions on constructing and perfecting the mechanism and policy framework of integrated urban and rural development system.*" It cites the imbalance between urban and rural areas—and the underdevelopment of rural areas—as the main "contradiction" of society. The long-established dual household *hukou* registration system and the dual welfare system attached to it have caused hundreds of millions of migrant workers to hover between urban and rural classification. They not only affect the healthy development of urbanization, but also slow the increase in agricultural labor productivity, ultimately holding back agriculture's comparative advantage and suppressing rural vitality (see Appendix).

In connection with the rural vitalization strategy, an integrated urban-rural development strategy has been formulated (CCCPC and State Council 2019).

By 2022, the strategy aims to establish mechanisms for implementing the integrated urban and rural development strategy, including opening channels of urban and rural factor movement, which requires removing barriers for migrated workers to gain *hukou* status in cities; integrated urban and rural land use markets; rural financial services supporting rural vitalization; protecting rural property and property transactions; equitable distribution of public services between rural and urban areas; and improved rural governance.

The rural vitalization strategy requires closing significant rural-urban gaps. These include establishing a long-term funding mechanism to support rural vitalization, attracting rural resident participation, upgrading rural industries, strengthening rural governance, and enhancing rural green development. If these mechanism are well established and implemented, an urban-rural migration system will be largely established, the urban-rural unified construction land market fully formed, the urban-rural inclusive financial service system fully established, public services basically equalized, the rural governance system improved, and agricultural and rural modernization may largely be achieved as envisaged.

Promotion of rural tourism

Tourism holds great potential to boost rural economic growth and environmental protection.

The integrated urban–rural development strategy and rural vitalization strategy promote economic activities that help diversify rural incomes and improve local infrastructure, landscape, and general living conditions. In recent years, people have found new interest in experiencing ecological agriculture and creative agriculture, along with rural sightseeing and leisure activities. Numerous agritainment and bed and breakfasts have opened. Rural tourism has gradually diversified, evolving from sightseeing to vacation-style "experience" tourism. For example, rural cultural tourism can focus on rural ethnic customs and traditional culture; while recreational tourism offers health benefits, wellness, fitness and entertainment.

Integrating agriculture and tourism diversifies farmer incomes and opens new income and employment opportunities. The Third National Agricultural Census (NBS 2017) in 2016 reported that 353,000 agricultural operators and operating units conducted new businesses such as catering, accommodation, harvesting, fishing, or simply experiencing agricultural life. These accounted for 5.9% of agricultural operating households and operating units. In 2018, there were 3 billion rural tourism excursions; about half of all domestic trips (Figure 8). Revenues reached some CNY800 billion, or 15.6% of tourist receipts (Figure 8). The government projects that 50 million farmers will be involved in rural tourism by 2020.[8]

While rural tourism has grown rapidly in recent years; its value-added lags behind other forms of tourism. In 2012, rural tourism accounted for 10.6% of domestic tourism revenue, rising only slowly to just 15.6% in 2018 (Figure 9).

Protection of the rural environment

Despite recent progress, challenges remain in managing the conversion of cultivated land for construction, avoiding water pollution, and promoting policies against non-point source pollution.

While agriculture has seen sustained growth over the past four decades, the intensive use of chemical fertilizers, pesticides, plastic mulch, untreated livestock and poultry waste, and burning crop residue resulted in ecological and environmental damage (such as soil pollution and degradation, surface water and aquifer pollution, air pollution, and eutrophication, among others). Untreated domestic waste from rural households exacerbated the impact. For instance, during 1986–2013, nitrogen use increased from 105 kilograms (kg) per hectare to 287.6 kg per hectare, while phosphate inputs increased from

---

8   Source: Further Promotion of Tourism Investment and Consumption; http://www.gov.cn/zhengce/content/2015-08/11/content_10075.htm.

Figure 8: Rural Tourism and Domestic Tourism, 2012–2019

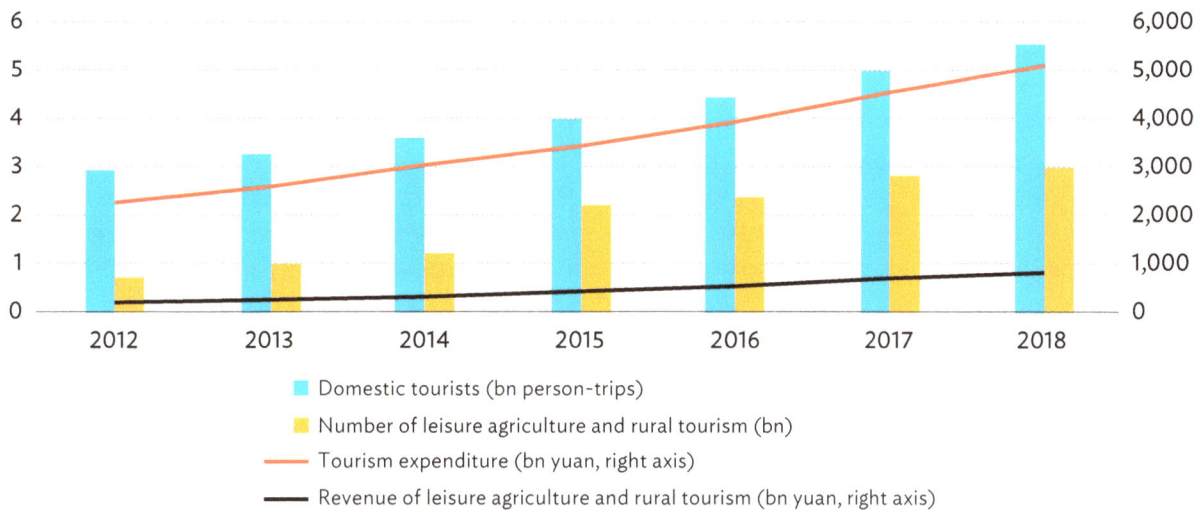

- Domestic tourists (bn person-trips)
- Number of leisure agriculture and rural tourism (bn)
- Tourism expenditure (bn yuan, right axis)
- Revenue of leisure agriculture and rural tourism (bn yuan, right axis)

Note: Tourism expenditure refers to expenses incurred during domestic travel, including transportation, tours, excursions, accommodation, dining, shopping, and entertainment.
Source: China Statistical Yearbook.

Figure 9: Share of Rural Tourism to Total Tourism

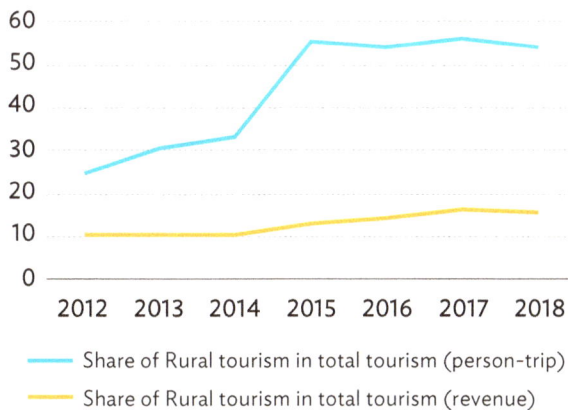

- Share of Rural tourism in total tourism (person-trip)
- Share of Rural tourism in total tourism (revenue)

Note: Tourism and rural tourism figures are defined as person-trips. Tourism expenditure refers to expenses incurred during domestic travel, including transportation, tours, excursions, accommodation, dining, shopping, and entertainment.
Source: China Statistical Yearbook.

23.3 to 92 kg per hectare. By 2017, fertilizer use reached 58.6 million tons, 41% more than in 2000. In fact, increased nutrient use exceeded yield growth—a possible indication of diminishing marginal returns of fertilizer use and low effective nutrient utilization. In 2017, the effective utilization ratio of fertilizers on rice, maize and wheat production was 37.8%, implying the majority of nutrients were released into soil and water, degrading soil and increasing pollution, along with the eutrophication of surface water. Similarly, increased pesticide use threatens agriculture sustainability by polluting water systems and jeopardizing human health and the ecosystem.

The PRC's use of chemical pesticides has been steadily increasing since the early 1990s, rising from 775.4 thousand tons in 1990 to 1.7 million tons in 2016, in parallel with the upward trend in crop production. Pesticide use (as measured by active ingredients) per hectare rose from about 5.9 kg in 1990 to 14.8 kg in 2012, before dropping to 13.1 kg in 2017. Another source of environmental damage from agriculture comes from the widespread use of plastic film and plastic mulch in vegetable and crop production—most of which is non-degradable plastic and mulch. Given available technology, it is often too costly to systematically recycle these plastics. Instead, they are frequently left on fields or burned with crop residue, thereby adding to the damaging environmental impact. In recent decades, rising demand for animal-based food products and increased domestic livestock and poultry production contributed much to water and soil pollution and raised greenhouse gas emissions.

In recent years, an institutional and policy framework has been established to improve the agricultural and rural environment. These include (i) protecting and rehabilitating agricultural land resources; (ii) regulations on the use of chemical fertilizers, pesticides and other chemicals; and (iii) protecting agricultural water resources. Economic mechanisms were introduced, covering the use of subsidies and sustainable cost recovery models in sanitation and rural wastewater financing. Community involvement has been enhanced—such as engaging local owners, outlining their roles and responsibilities, and boosting their technical capacity.

Land Protection

Protecting agricultural land resources and their sustainable use has been central to PRC policy making. The Outline of the National Overall Planning on Land Use (2006–2020)—compiled by the Ministry of Land and Resources and approved by the State Council—specifies overall planning targets, the main implementation tasks, and specific regulations covering agricultural land protection and use. It states that 1.8 billion mu[9] (120 million hectare) of cultivated land must be protected, of which 1.6 billion mu are considered

as the "basic agricultural land" to be better maintained. By 2020, cultivated land converted for construction purposes will be limited to 45 million mu. Land consolidation, rehabilitation and development should provide additional cultivated land of at least 55 million mu.

"Basic ecological land" will also be strictly protected to ensure that cultivated land, grazing and grassland, water areas, and certain unutilized lands ecologically important must exceed 75% of total national land. The Outline calls for improving the ecological environment by, for example, maintenance of retired cultivated land, rehabilitation and reclamation of wasteland from industry and mining activities, and the treatment of degraded land.

Efforts to protect agricultural and ecological land resources target both the "quantity" and the "quality" of resources as well as their long-term sustainability. The No. 1 central document of 2015 (CCCPC and State Council 2015a) includes an action plan for protecting and upgrading the quality of arable land. Strengthening farmland ecological protection, and boosting improvement and restoration work on degraded, polluted, and damaged farmland are outlined in the "Opinions on Speeding up the Construction of Ecological Civilization" by the CCCPC and State Council (2015b).

Reducing use of chemical fertilizers and pesticides

The 2020 Zero-Growth Action Plan for Pesticides (MOA 2015) is designed to reduce chemical fertilizer and pesticide use. It restricts annual growth of chemical fertilizer use to less than 1% during 2015–2019 and to reach zero-growth by 2020 for major agricultural crops. Implementation details vary by region given the different levels of fertilizer use. For instance, in regions overusing chemical fertilizers, such as Northeastern PRC, the Northern Plain, and mid- and lower Yangtze River region, nitrogen and phosphorus inputs were to be either controlled or reduced, with the use of potassium

---

9   A mu is a Chinese unit of measurement (1 mu = 666.67 m²).

stabilized. In Southwestern PRC, nitrogen use would be stabilized, the use of phosphorus fertilizers adjusted, with potassium use increased. In Northwestern PRC, fertilizer and water resource use were to be balanced, with nitrogen and phosphorus use stabilized (MOA 2015).

Similarly, as excessive pesticide use both increases production costs, affects food safety, and damages the ecological system, action plan targets zero-growth by 2020. The plan emphasizes green prevention and control on pest, professional pest control, and scientific application of pesticides.

The declared goals have all been achieved. For chemical fertilizers, data from China Statistics Yearbooks show that annual growth of fertilizer use has in fact fallen since 2016, whereas pesticides met the zero annual growth target in 2014. Nonetheless, the level of chemical fertilizer and pesticide use remains high, requiring continuous efforts to shift to more sustainable production practices.

Control of water pollution

Agriculture causes water pollution due to its improper use of chemical fertilizers, waste from livestock and poultry, along with untreated household waste. Excessive nutrient pollution leads to persistent eutrophication of surface water. During 2006–2011, roughly half of the PRC's major lakes and reservoirs were in some state of eutrophication (China Environmental Bulletin 2007–2018). Since 2012, monitoring and testing has been expanded to cover 109 key lakes and reservoirs, with 14–35 in various degrees of eutrophication (though none were considered severely eutrophicated).

A Water Pollution Prevention and Control Action Plan issued by the State Council in 2015 focused on protecting water resources. First, the areas

prohibiting livestock and poultry breeding are scientifically defined. Large scale operations, including intensive backyard livestock and poultry activities, must have complementary pollution and waste storage, processing, and reutilization facilities. Second, agricultural non-point pollution from the use of fertilizers and pesticides had to be controlled. Aside from supporting the use of low-toxicity pesticides and applying soil testing formula fertilization, environmental requirements covered construction on high standard farmland and on land consolidation and exploitation. Third, nationwide adjustments were made on the structure and spatial distribution of various crops: retiring land in water-deficient regions, cultivating crops requiring less fertilizer and pesticides, and reducing cultivated areas of water-intensive crops. By the end of 2018, comprehensive changes were to be made on 33 million mu (2.2 million hectares) of irrigated farmland to save more than 3.7 billion cubic meters of water.

The action plan improved water quality. According to the Ministry of Ecology and Environment,[10] by the end of 2019, more than 263,000 livestock and poultry farms (communities) in prohibited areas were closed or relocated. Comprehensive rural environmental projects were carried out in 188,000 villages. Drinking water protection had been strengthened in 2,804 water sources, improving drinking water safety and quality for 770 million residents. In 2019, the proportion of nationally controlled sections of surface water with good water quality was 74.9%, an increase of 8.9 percentage points from 2015.

Preventing non-point source pollution from agriculture

Agricultural non-point source pollution policies consist of economic incentives and guidelines and, more importantly, direct control policies. The "Agricultural Environment Management

Regulations" in 1988 began the systematic monitoring of agricultural pollution and regulating agricultural production for environmental protection. In July 2004, the prevention and control of non-point source pollution was officially launched in line with the goals of increased agricultural production and farmer income—under the principle of "reduction, reuse, and recycle."

In 2012 and 2014, the PRC formally established a policy framework for the regulation of systematic agricultural non-point source pollution prevention and control, and defined agricultural non-point source pollution prevention goals as "one control" (control of total agricultural water consumption and agricultural water pollution), "two reductions" (reduction in the use of chemical fertilizers and pesticides) and "three basics" (basic resource utilization, comprehensive recycling and harmless treatment of livestock and poultry waste and pollution, agricultural film and crop straws). After the PRC formally put the prevention and control of agricultural non-point source pollution on the policy agenda, it immediately introduced relevant policies.

While establishing guiding principles, action plans, regulations and implementation documents suggest a strong policy framework is being put in place, economic incentives are also needed so farmers can adopt more sustainable agricultural production practices.

Promoting the "circular economy" and "environmental business"

Along with tougher environmental protection regulations, the circular economy concept has received increasing attention as a way to prevent the further deterioration of the agricultural environment, while maintaining sustainable agricultural development. It means optimizing use of idle resources and wastes. The private sector has been tapped as a mechanism to recover additional costs associated with environmental action. Eco-labelling and ecotourism also allow rural areas to internalize the cost of additional environmental action.

An agricultural circular economy involves the cultivation of crops, animal husbandry, reprocessing agriculture waste, and other farm management and marketing activities. Developing circular agriculture requires the combination of human, animal, and agricultural waste into organic resources to generate biogas, fertilizers and other materials.

Despite the development of circular agriculture in households, the rural circular economy remains small and involves relatively few cross-sectoral or cross-regional partners. Even with government support, there are relatively few examples of private business involvement that leveraged under-utilized resources into larger and more efficient circular agricultural activities. Future development should therefore focus on generating incentives that attract public and private investment and innovation to scale up the agricultural circular economy.

Policy Implications

The PRC has programs that address rural vulnerability—such as rural vitalization and rural-urban development integration; it targets the overall revitalization of the village by the mid- 21st century.

The PRC has officially eradicated absolute rural poverty through a series of extensive reforms in landownership and use, increased investments in modernizing agricultural infrastructure to diversify economic activities and raise rural incomes, and in expanding rural public services. However, the rural-urban income disparity remains a major concern. As mentioned, in 2018 the average per capita urban income was 2.7 times that in rural areas. The rural population continues to decline and is set to age rapidly.

The expansion of agricultural production driven by intensive use of chemicals has caused environmental degradation. Economic growth in rural area can no longer be achieved at the expense of sustainable use of natural resources and requires more resilience to climate change. Going forward, enhancing environmental welfare is key for rural areas to be attractive places to live, visit, and launch entrepreneurial activities. To that end, more investment is needed in rural environmental infrastructure, such as waste management, landscape and ecotourism facilities. With continuing reforms, the PRC is positioned to play a leading role in establishing a model of sustainable rural development in the Asia and Pacific region.

Four features of the PRC's rural development provide important lessons for developing Asia.

Flexible, Adaptive Policies

The government adjusted rural development policy strategies to fit rapidly evolving socio-economic situations. For example, No. 1 central documents have been annually updating policy priorities for rural development for the past 14 years. Policy reforms in the late 1970s focused on boosting food production and maintaining grain self-sufficiency. The policy evolved in the mid-1990s to increase competitiveness of the rural economy through agricultural modernization and economic diversification. Since the 2010s, rural policy has shifted to a more integrated and balanced approach to improve economic, social and environmental welfare. Support to agriculture refocused to ensuring long-term food security through sustainable use of natural resources.

Innovative Institutions

Innovations were introduced in rural land use and the reorganization of small-scale farms. A household responsibility system that originated in the late 1970s allocated land contract rights to individual households, which initially boosted agriculture production in early 1980s, but created a small and fragmented farm structure. Since the 2000s, a variety of institutional innovations have consolidated small-scale operations into larger units. The holders of land contract rights were allowed to lease their land operational rights, raising rural incomes.

The emergence of farm mechanization service providers enabled small-scale farmers to quickly mechanize cultivation without heavy capital investment. Mechanization reduced labor inputs for farming and increased time available for off-farm income opportunities. Voluntary cooperative organizations provided a range of services to connect small-scale farmers to markets and the latest technologies through training, and collective marketing and input supply. Some cooperative organizations consolidated land operational rights from member farmers to form a single farm management unit. All these institutional innovations are highly relevant for other countries with a small and fragmented farm structure.

Infrastructure Investments

Network infrastructure investments in rural areas include roads, the telephone system, and internet on top of developing basic agricultural infrastructure such as irrigation and drainage. It connected farmers to markets and enabled manufacturing and service industries to develop in rural areas. High internet and mobile network penetration in rural areas accelerated the application of ICT. E-commerce platforms such as Taobao have been essential in connecting farmers to end-consumers and oriented agriculture to be more demand-driven.

E-commerce has played a significant role in maintaining food supply chains during the COVID-19 pandemic. Beyond providing a platform for transactions, e-commerce platforms invested in logistics and marketing infrastructure and provided training for farmers to adopt new technologies. The growing engagement of technology companies in rural development is providing a new model of development, led by the private sector.

Strong Social Protection

Rural health insurance and pensions have improved since the early 2000s to help bridge the gap with the urban social protection system. A rural minimum basic living guarantee (*Dibao*) provides unconditional cash transfers to the poor (6.2% of the rural population as of April 2019). Since 2017 rural *Dibao* standard—a per capita income threshold below which residents are entitled to receive payments—has met or exceeded the national poverty alleviation standards in all the counties (cities, districts, and banners) across the country. An expanded social protection system has improved the quality of life in rural areas, and assisted elderly farmers retire and transfer their farm assets to more efficient operators.

DEVELOPING SUSTAINABLE ELDERLY CARE SYSTEM

5

The PRC Experience

With an aging population, it is imperative that the PRC allocate greater resources to address elderly care.

Over time, aging can hurt an economy as a rising share of elderly can reduce the labor force and output per adult. Social security expenditures also rise. Appropriate policies can increase resources to respond to the rise in the number of elderly and also to partly offset the labor squeeze.

In its early years, the major efforts of the government in addressing population aging were focused on establishing social security systems and expanding coverage. Social security policies for the elderly mainly include pensions and social assistance, which aim to provide adequate retirement income to maintain quality of life and prevent poverty in old age. Pensions are typically funded by contributions made by employees and employers, and sometimes with government subsidies. Social assistance is government-funded cash or in-kind benefits provided to people usually meeting a set of means-test criteria. Internationally, while pension systems in most countries continue to undergo active reforms to improve financial sustainability and increase coverage as populations age, social assistance is receiving increased attention (in both developed and developing countries) as a way to address remaining poverty and security gaps. In countries where long-term care insurance is not used, such as the PRC, pensions and social assistance

are often the major sources of income to access elderly care services.

It was not until the early 2010s when increased emphasis was given to developing an elderly care system. As a developing and middle-income economy, the phenomenon of rapid population aging has been often discussed in terms of "aging before getting rich". In this context, providing affordable care services from the perspective of both the government and older people has been a major issue in developing the PRC's elderly care system.

The PRC's policies that address the effects of an aging population are based on experience, as described below.

How an Aging Population Leads to Vulnerability

Poverty among the elderly has been persistent.

By the end of 2020, 3.7 million rural and 0.2 million urban elderly received Assistance for People with Special Difficulties, while 1.5 million urban and 13.4 million rural elderly received *Dibao* benefits (or 18.4% and 37% of *Dibao* recipients, respectively). This amounts to 22.7 million elderly living in poverty, or 9% of the population over 60 years old. If this trend continues, the size of the vulnerable elderly population will increase.

Social security policies for the elderly include pensions and social assistance. Shortly after the economic reforms of the early 1980s, the

This chapter draws on the background paper prepared by Yuebin, Xu (Xu 2021).

old-age pension system began to be reformed and became a major policy in providing social security for the elderly. The emergence of urban poverty due to layoffs by state-owned enterprises in the mid 1990s left many people with no access to social insurance protection. Toward the end of the 20th century, the government's attention was drawn to social assistance as a way to address poverty for people not covered by social insurance.

Pensions

With an aging population, the elderly have become increasingly vulnerable to poverty because pension and social assistance resources are overextended.

The basic pension system includes two schemes based on occupational status. One is the Urban Employees' Basic Pension System (UEBPS), established in the early 1990s. It gradually expanded to cover all employees with formal labor contracts, including employees in government departments, public institutions, and workers in enterprises. The program is funded with pay-as-you-go social pooling plus funded individual accounts. Social pooling includes employers, who contribute a maximum 16%, and individuals, who contribute 8% of wages. After contributing at least 15 years, a worker reaching retirement age (60 for men and 55 for women) receives a monthly basic pension. By the end of 2018, UEBPS had about 420 million participants with 118 million retirees, or 50.3% of the urban population.

The second scheme is the Residents Basic Pension System (RBPS), which covers people not covered by UEBPS. RBPS was established for rural residents in 2009 and for urban residents in 2011. It is funded by government subsidies and individual contributions. Twelve levels of individual contributions range from an annual amount of CNY100 to CNY2,000, with participants allowed to select which level. Benefits have two tiers—a basic pension and individual account pension. Funding of the basic pension is shared by the central and local

governments. The central government determines the minimum amount of subsidies on an annual basis, while local governments can raise the subsidy level on their own. Individual contributions and the portion of subsidies contributed by local governments are held in individual accounts, while subsidies from the central government and a portion of local government subsidies make up the basic pension. A participant reaching age 60 after contributing for 15 years would receive a fixed amount from the basic pension and a monthly sum equal to 1/139 of the funds accumulated in the individual account. This has led to wide disparities in the amount of both basic pensions and individual account pensions across the country. A special feature of the scheme is that all elderly are eligible for the basic pension, regardless whether they have contributed to the scheme or not, which allows it to operate like a social pension system. By the end of 2018, RBPS enrolled about 524 million participants with 159 million people receiving benefits.

In 2018, the PRC had 277 million pensioners, or about 20% of the total population, with 57% drawing pensions from RBPS and 43% from UEBP. As provincially unified schemes, pension benefits vary markedly across schemes and provinces. Nationally, in 2016, the monthly pension for retirees of enterprises averaged CNY2,362, while that for RBPS participants averaged CNY105 for the basic pension.

Social Assistance

The PRC's social assistance system provides a variety of means-tested cash and/or in-kind benefits for low-income and poverty-stricken households. It covers basic living, medical care, education, housing and employment, among others. Three programs are eligible to the elderly and their families—Assistance for People with Special Difficulties (APSD), Minimum Living Standard Guarantee Scheme (*Dibao*), and Allowances for the Senior Elderly.

APSD provides cash benefits and care services to those without family caregivers and sources of income. It originated from two social assistance schemes established in the 1950s for rural Five-Guarantees and urban Three-Nos (Inability to work, no source of income, no legal supporter or the obligor of support, or the supporter is indeed incapable of support or the obligor of support has not performed the obligation). Following the State Council 2014 Interim Regulations on Social Assistance, the two schemes were merged into APSD, while the Five-Guarantees and Three-Nos were combined into People with Special Difficulties (PSD). Eligible people include orphans aged below 16 and the elderly and disabled who are unable to provide for themselves through work, and cannot obtain support from family caregivers. Benefits include cash assistance and care services. Depending on their physical condition, PSD can be helped either through cash assistance if they live at their own homes or by placing them in a public residential care (RC) facility established especially for PSD in townships and street offices. By the end of 2020, APSD covered 3.7 million rural and 0.2 million urban elderly.

Dibao is to provide a minimum living guarantee for family members living together whose per capita income is lower than the local subsistence standard and whose property status meets the requirements. The identification of *Dibao* families is based on three elements: household registration status, family income and family property. Family members living together include spouses, parents and minor children, children who have grown up but cannot live independently, and other persons who have legal support and support obligations and been living together for a long time. As of the end of 2020, *Dibao* covers urban populations of 8.1 million and rural populations of 36.2 million; urban subsistence allowance per capita monthly subsidy of 476 yuan (approximately 21% of urban residents' consumption expenditure), and rural subsistence

allowance per capita of 295 yuan (approximately 26% of rural residents' consumption expenditure). As of the end of 2020, about 33.6% of the elderly enjoy the subsistence allowance.

Allowances for the Senior Elderly began in several municipalities around 2000 (Tianjin in 1999). It was adopted nationally in 2016. In most places, the program provides a monthly fixed amount of cash benefits for those over 80 years, paid either as a universal benefit (in Beijing, CNY100 is paid monthly to those aged 90-99 and CNY200 to those over 100 years old), or just to those living with *Dibao* or low-income households (such as in Fujian Province where those aged 80 or above receive CNY100 monthly).

The medical care insurance system consists of two basic medical insurance systems: (i) the Employees' Basic Medical Insurance System (EBMI), and (ii) the Residents' Basic Medical Insurance System (RBMI). In 2019, the reimbursement rate within the scope of medical insurance policy was reported at above 80% of total EBMI medical care costs, while it was 70% of total inpatient costs through RBMI.[11]

Development of the Elderly Care System

To complement social security and social organizations for the older generation, the PRC developed an Elderly Care System that relies on both government and private sector support.

The Three-tiered System

As early as 2000, the central government began to explore the establishment of an elderly care system—consisting of home and community-based care (HCBC) and residential care. This developed into a three-tiered system defined

---

11   NHSA. 2020. "Statistical Communique for development of basic medical care security system in 2019", http://www.nhsa.gov.cn/art/2020/6/24/art_7_3268.html (accessed 11 January 2021).

in the Twelfth Five Year Plan (2011–2015) as "home-based care as core support, community-based care as necessary support, and RC as supplementary support". The plan also set specific targets: (i) the number of RC beds would reach 30 per 1,000 elderly; (ii) home-based care should cover all urban communities, 80% of rural townships and 50% of villages; and (iii) the development of community-based care—day care centers and other types of community-based elderly care services—should be strengthened. The targets were restated in State Council 2013 *"Opinions on Speeding up Development of Elderly Care Services"*, with 30–40 RC beds per 1,000 elderly and coverage of home-based care in all urban communities, 90% of townships and 60% of villages by 2020. The Thirteenth Five-Year Plan (2016–2020) continued with the three-tiered system while it merged "home-based care" and "community-based care" into HCBC. It also promoted establishing an integrated health and elderly care system and strengthened private sector involvement in elderly care investment. Thus, building an elderly care system (consisting of RC and HCBC) with integrated medical care and a pluralistic delivery system has been the major theme guiding elderly care service development.

This type of elderly care system is obviously in the right direction and consistent with international practices that emphasize HCBC. Implementation, however, has been unbalanced, with RC receiving substantially more government funding. Combined with the elderly's limited resources to purchase care services, it has led to an oversupply of RC beds (empty beds) and generally underdeveloped HCBC.

Residential Care

RC refers to elderly care services provided by a residential facility for those residing in the facility round-the-clock. Apart from boarding services, an RC facility typically provides health-care services and other support depending on resident needs. Before the 1990s, almost all RC facilities were publicly run, providing care to those living on social welfare free of charge, including "Three Nos" and "Five Guarantees". Since the early 1990s, most government efforts have focused on developing and reforming RC facilities. Starting in the early 1990s, public welfare institutions generated income by providing services to self-paying residents. This led to a rapid increase in the number of self-paying elderly (now the majority) in public RC facilities.

Beginning in the early 2010s, the central government issued a series of policies to reform public RC facilities and to promote private involvement in delivering elderly care services. This has transformed public RC facilities into broadly three types: (i) public (government funded and operated); (ii) publicly funded and privately operated; and (iii) nongovernment facilities (privately funded and operated, public institutions, and communities, among others). In 2019, among registered RC facilities, the number of nongovernment RC facilities and RC beds accounted for 40%–45% of RC facilities and beds respectively. Public RC facilities are a safety net for the indigent poor. They are required to prioritize dependent or semi-dependent elderly with financial difficulties. Public RC facilities include social welfare institutions in cities and homes for the aged in the countryside. Urban RCs provide care for the Three Nos while also accept fee-paying elderly. Countryside RCs care for Five Guarantee households. Publicly funded and privately operated facilities accept both social welfare recipients and the self-paying elderly, while private RC facilities are expected to mainly accept the self-paying elderly.

Home and Community-based Care

HCBC refers to community-based elderly care facilities—including day care centers and home delivery services—in support of the elderly living in their own homes. Although the development of HCBCs began in the early 2000s and was emphasized in the two 5-year plans in developing elderly care services, progress has been slow with both supply and utilization of services limited.

Recent pilots of HCBC services started in 2016 with an annual CNY1 billion from the central government. By 2019, four rounds of pilots had been carried out, covering 142 cities and districts/townships. The pilot cities were allowed to use funds to develop HCBC in several ways: (i) attracting private involvement in elderly care through purchasing services or establishing various public-private partnerships (PPP); (ii) supporting RC facilities to deliver HCBC; (iii) applying "Internet Plus" in HCBCs; (iv) training caregivers; (v) improving care quality and monitoring; (vi) exploring ways to integrate medical and care services; and (vii) increasing the supply of elderly care facilities. Pilot localities were to serve as demonstration projects to advance HCBC development nationwide. Between 2015 and 2018, the number of various HCBC facilities increased from 88,000 to 136,000.

Along with piloting HCBC in more cities, in 2019 the Ministry of Civil Affairs (MCA) set a target that, by 2022, all street offices establish at least one comprehensive community-based elderly care facility able to provide both RC and HCBC services and offer HCBC guidance. Each community should also set up a day care center to provide services, such as daily care, meals, emergency help, recreational activities, and social support. The document requires over 90% of urban communities to have these facilities, with rural townships also working to establish these facilities when conditions allow.

Health and Care Integration

Integrating medical care and nursing services has been promoted by the government since the early 2010s. Early on, large public RC facilities were encouraged to run clinics to provide medical care for residents, and community health facilities were asked to provide basic health care—such as health

management or keeping health records—for the elderly. This was followed by the requirement that local governments direct medical care resources into RC facilities, communities and families, and explore ways for hospitals to collaborate with RC facilities and provide home delivery health care. A major policy issued by 10 ministries in 2015 said that, by 2020, all medical care facilities should have a green channel for the elderly to receive medical care services, and that all RC facilities make needed medical services accessible to residents. Several ways to integrate health and care services were explored: (i) RC facilities collaborating with medical and health institutions; (ii) RC facilities setting up medical care services or clinics; and (iii) medical and health institutions extending services to communities and families. These were further promoted in the Thirteenth Five-Year Plan and through several government policies.

The 2016 Healthy PRC 2030 Plan and its implementation plan promoted the idea of active aging and prevention through health-care extension to communities and families. While earlier measures focused on medical and RC institutions, the new policy emphasized services to the active and independent elderly in communities and families, requiring community health centers and family doctors to play a major role in promoting good health for all.

Private Sector Participation

Encouraging private investment in establishing a pluralistic elderly care service delivery system has been a government policy theme since the early 2000s. Earlier policies encouraged private investment through preferential policies such as free land allocation, exemption of taxes and fees, lower utility costs and promoting public–private partnerships by contracting out public RC facilities for private operation. In the early 2010s, population aging was viewed as a market opportunity, and a set of new policies was issued by different ministries to require local governments to provide preferential policies to encourage both private and foreign investment in elderly care, and prioritize private capital in building new facilities. The private sector was encouraged to engage in a wide array of elderly care services, ranging from meal services to home delivery medical care and local infrastructure, such as home modification and barrier-free reconstruction in communities and rural areas.

A typical example is that of the HCBC project in Zhanggong District, Ganzhou, Jiangxi Province which has brought in professional private capital through the PPP model; improved the facilities to become more elderly-friendly from the perspective of users; adopted the tiered pricing model; and provided a variety of customized services such as day care, 24-hour care, cultural and recreational services, housekeeping, meal and bath assistance, emergency and medical services with the help of the 'smart community' senior care service platform. About 110,000 elderly people over 60 years old in the district have received all-round, personalization and intelligent services from both physical and mental levels; practical problems that are difficult to solve in traditional community senior care have been solved.

The most recent tax concessions for the elderly care sector were aimed specially to boost HCBC by reducing service providers' financial burden and encouraging private elderly care investment. A series of financial incentives were offered for HCBC providers, including (i) revenues from services exempted from value added tax, with all providers eligible for a 10% deduction in taxable income; and (ii) real estate or land used for providing services exempted from deed tax, property tax, land use tax, and various fees such as urban infrastructure fee and real estate registration fee.

Despite increasing financial incentives for private providers, two main issues remain: (i) direct supply side subsidies may not necessarily contribute to increasing effective demand, particularly from the vast majority of the low and

middle-income elderly population; the generally low occupancy rate in most private RC facilities will likely lead to low or uncertain returns on investment—a major factor in deterring the private sector from entering the industry; and (ii) with most private and public elderly care facilities allowed to accept able-bodied elderly— based on their ability to pay rather than their care needs—public finance tends to go to those without or few care needs, leading to low resource allocation efficiency.

Financing

Elderly care financing has both supply- and demand-side components.

Funding for the development and operation of the elderly care system comes mainly from three sources: government revenues, public welfare lottery funds, and social donations. Among them, government revenues have been used mainly to cover the construction and operation of public RC facilities, such as urban social welfare institutions and rural homes for the aged, and funding responsibilities are borne mainly by local governments with occasional central transfers. Public welfare lottery funds include central and local welfare lottery funds and the central special public welfare lottery funds, which have been used to support public welfare projects in various fields, including elderly care services. Social donations include government charities such as the China Charity Federation and China Social Welfare Foundation, with funds usually allocated on a project basis. Apart from these funding sources, preferential policies on land use, taxation and fees and use of utilities have been used since the early 1990s for both public and private facilities.

While public elderly care facilities are fully funded by government revenues, subsidies have been the major way to encourage the private sector to invest in or run elderly care services. Starting in the early 2010s, the central government asked local governments to subsidize the construction and operation of private RC facilities, based on either service capacity or utilization. Local governments have discretion over the form subsidies take based on the local situation.[12] Since 2016, the central government has used a performance-based approach to determine the level of central transfers for provinces. They include indicators such as the average number of beds per thousand elderly people, percentage of nursing beds to total beds, and the construction of elderly care facilities in previous and current years.[13]

Local governments use a performance-based strategy and developed various schemes to provide subsidies to their elderly care facilities. The subsidies are funded mainly by local governments, usually shared between municipal and district/county governments, while transfers from the central government are made increasingly available. Overall, subsidies for the construction and operation of elderly care facilities are generally available in most provinces and cities, while other types of subsidies are provided in some localities with varying designs. As one of the richest cities in the PRC, Hangzhou provided more subsidies than Wuhan for construction with more funding for non-profit facilities and for those providing nursing care (Table 3). Wuhan is also a high-income city. While it does not differentiate for-profit and non-profit construction subsidies, it also encourages those able to care for those elderly who are dependent. However, a needs assessment is required to ensure public supported facilities provide a mix of services and meet the elderly care needs efficiently.

On the demand side, since 2014, cash subsidies have been provided to the elderly with both care needs and financial difficulty.[14] With local governments responsible for funding subsidies, eligibility and subsidy levels vary markedly across provinces and cities. In 2018, about 6 million old people received subsidies for elderly care services.[15] Compared with subsidies on the supply side, subsidies for the elderly using services are limited in both scope and subsidy amount. For example, in Chengdu, eligible elderly people include those from *Dibao* and low-income households, while in Wuhan only the elderly with special difficulties are eligible for subsidies (Table 4). Similar to other localities, those elderly other than the most destitute must pay for services. Given the low pensions most old people receive, many cannot afford elderly care services.

In sum, establishing a pluralistic and three-tiered elderly care system was adopted by government to meet the care needs of a rapidly aging population. Efforts have focused on increasing the supply of elderly care services by promoting private involvement through preferential treatment and subsidies, and on the demand side, by ensuring care for the most destitute is guaranteed through means-tested schemes. Thus, while the government has been increasing financial incentives for service providers, subsidies on the demand side are limited both in scope and amount. For most of the elderly with care needs, access to formal elderly care services depends largely on their ability to pay.

---

[12] State Council (2010) *"Opinions on encouraging and guiding private capital to enter the elderly care service industry"*; MOCA (2012) *"Opinions on implementing policies for encouraging and guiding private capital to enter the elderly care service industry"*, http://www.gov.cn/zhengce/2016-05/22/content_5075659.htm (accessed 14 April 2020).

[13] NDRC (2016) "Circular on methods of providing central subsidies for supporting elderly care development", http://www.gov.cn/xinwen/2016-12/30/content_5154994.htm (accessed 15 April 2020).

[14] Ministry of Finance, MOCA and NCOA (2014) "Circular on providing subsidies for old people with advanced age and financial difficulties", http://www.gov.cn/xinwen/2014-10/23/content_2769678.htm (accessed 14 October 2020).

[15] MoCA (2019) "Statistical Communiqué of Social Service Development in 2018", http://images3.mca.gov.cn/www2017/file/201908/1565920301578.pdf (accessed 14 April 2020).

Table 3: Subsidies for Private Elderly Care Facilities in Hangzhou and Wuhan in 2018

Subsidies	Cities	
	Hangzhou	Wuhan
RC facilities		
Construction (lump sum)	CNY5,000–12,000/per bed for non-profit facilities depending on location and property type (rental or owned); 80% of the above rate for for-profit facilities; additional subsidies of CNY1,000–4,000 for facilities with nursing care beds depending on property type and location; 20% increase in budget for new public facilities approved for establishment (maximum CNY3 million).	CNY5,000–8000/per bed for non-profit facilities depending on property type (rental or owned); same rates for for-profit facilities and rural welfare homes (public) if they admit and provide care to dependent elderly.
Operation (monthly)	CNY200 for each independent elderly over 80 and CNY600 for each dependent elderly receiving care.	CNY200 for each independent, and CNY300 for each dependent elderly receiving care.
HCBC facilities (including rural and urban elderly care service centers, day care centers, and care stations)		
Construction (Lump sum)	Subsidies such as for day care centers, meal services, and other services are provided by district governments, based on performance scores.	CNY30,000–150,000 for different types of facilities
Operation (annually)		CNY20,000–100,000 for different types of facilities
Other subsidies		
	CNY100,000–150,000 lump sum for facilities running medical services depending on scale of medical service; CNY10,000–50,000 for private facilities being ranked above 3 stars in the star classification system (1–5 stars); Subsidies for coverage of elderly care facilities by insurances for contingencies	Lump sum CNY200,000 for brand building for chain operators with more than 10 facilities; Lump sum CNY0.5–1 million construction subsidies for elderly care operating within communities (community-imbedded elderly care)

RC = residential care; HCBC = home and community-based care.
Sources: Hangzhou Municipal Civil Affairs Bureau and Hangzhou Municipal Finance Bureau. 2019. "Methods for implementing subsidies for EC services in Hangzhou", http://www.hangzhou.gov.cn/art/2019/4/1/art_1636467_4550.html;(accessed 9 October 2020) and Wuhan Municipal Civil Affairs Bureau. 2017. *"Opinions on increasing supply of and speeding up EC services"*, http://mzj.wuhan.gov.cn/zwgk_918/fdzdgk/gysyjs/shfl/201708/t20170823_1000655.shtml (accessed 27 November 2020).

Table 4: Subsidies for Elderly Care Service Users in Chengdu and Wuhan

	Chengdu	Wuhan
Eligibilities	Elderly people from *Dibao* or low-income households	Elderly people from *Dibao* or low-income households; elderly people living in city central with pension income lower than the local average of the previous year; and elderly people receiving other preferential treatment policies
Amount	Monthly CNY50 for independent elderly; CNY300-CNY500 for elderly with moderate and severe disability; additional CNY200 if moving to live in residential care.	Monthly CNY100-CNY800 based on assessed level of functional ability.

Sources: Chengdu Municipal People's Government. 2018. http://gk.chengdu.gov.cn/govInfoPub/detail.action?id=102387&tn=6 (accessed 27 November 2020). Wuhan Municipal Civil Afafirs ciBureau. 2018b. http://mzj.wuhan.gov.cn/zwgk_918/zc/zcfg/202004/t20200416_1018732.shtml(accessed 27 November 2020).

Starting in 2016, long-term care insurance (LTCI) was piloted in 15 cities from 14 provinces or provincial-level municipalities. According to the *"Guiding Opinions on Piloting Long-Term Care Insurance"*,[16] the pilots had two objectives: (i) explore the establishment of a social insurance system in financing elderly care services and accumulate experience for developing LTCI policies for implementation during the 13th Five-Year Plan period (2016–2020); and (ii) explore policies related to the scope of LTCI coverage, premiums and benefits, and develop management tools such as needs assessment and quality management of care services. While local governments were given discretion in designing and implementing their own schemes, based on local circumstances, the guiding opinions laid out key policy parameters on the care services to be covered, target populations to be insured, financing mechanisms, and benefits.

Key Policy Recommendations

Policies should be designed to make elderly care sustainable by matching actual needs with available resources and strengthening the government's role.

Improve the Elderly Care System to Better Integrate RC and HCBC

The current elderly care system must improve to better integrate and balance HCBC and RC development. Specifically, the elderly care system should be designed with clearly defined service goals and targets based on the principle of "ageing in place", with RC and HCBC serving the elderly with different needs. Public RC facilities above the district/county level should be upgraded and developed with a focus on providing care mainly for those

with complex care needs—such as those with cognitive impairments or severe disabilities. Along with the improvement and increasing availability of HCBC, the care needs of the elderly with moderate impairments can usually be met in family or community settings, leading to the general reduction in demand for RC. However, the declining availability of adult children as family caregivers may increase the need for formal elderly care services such as day care services, respite care, family caregiver training and others to help families provide adequate care. In either case, demand for RC would be mainly for treating cases that cannot be effectively dealt with in family or community settings. Care for people with complex needs requires skilled and professional services, including medical and rehabilitation services, which can be provided more efficiently in a municipal institution, once equipped with assessment tools, standards, and skilled workforce.

The goal of HCBC is to keep the elderly in their family and community if possible by providing preventative care and services. A well-developed HCBC service system would enable the elderly with limited impairments to stay at home instead of moving into institutions. This is key to balanced elderly care development. Specifically, day care centers at the street office and/or township level should provide care for those with moderate impairments, either at the facility or through home delivered personal care or other care services. Community-based elderly care stations would mainly provide meals, housekeeping or other individualized services that do not need a highly skilled or professional workforce. Operating an elderly care system with integrated RC and HCBC development requires using a municipally unified needs assessment and referral system.

---

[16]   MHSS. 2016. *"Guiding opinions on piloting of long-term care insurances"*, http://www.gov.cn/xinwen/2016-07/08/content_5089283.htm (accessed April 2020).

Increase the Government's Financing Role

On the supply side, government subsidies should shift from subsidizing construction or operating RC beds to increasing payments to those working in RC facilities and day care centers—to ensure qualified nurses and caregivers receive adequate wages. Properly implemented, subsidies can achieve quality care without raising user service fees. Currently, many provinces and cities using subsidies for caregivers have various funding levels, although most subsidies remain low. This should be strengthened by sector through central transfers to facilitate development of elderly care human resources, particularly in poorer localities. As discussed earlier, the lack of RC facilities with both quality care and affordable fees has been a deterring factor for the elderly to use RC. Investing in skilled human resources would both have a long-term impact on service quality and lead to lower costs for service providers and fees for end-users.

On the demand side, a co-payment mechanism between government and those using elderly care services could increase the purchasing power of the elderly and their families for elderly care services. Specifically, a mix of fixed rate and means-tested subsidies should be used to cover all those with care needs. Fixed rate subsidies should be applied universally to those with assessed care needs for specified government financed services, regardless of financial capability.

For the elderly using RC, means-tested cost sharing by government can also ensure that those with mid- to low incomes can receive needed care. Currently, APSD recipients are fully funded and *Dibao* recipients partially funded by government when receiving RC. These subsidies can be expanded to those elderly drawing the generally low RBPS pensions. To contain costs and discourage the use of RC by those whose care needs can be met through HCBC or the family system, government subsidies should cover part of the costs of specified care services in proportion to incomes, while users should bear part of the cost of care services and all costs of room, board and other services not publicly financed.

Support Community and Non-profit Organizations in Providing HCBC

HCBC should be viewed and operated as a public benefit. It not only enhances the quality of life for the elderly, but also contributes to a reduction in RC use—which is more costly than HCBC for both the government and family. To make HCBC more affordable and accessible to all the elderly and their families, the government should be more active in financing. Specifically, it should support community and non-profit organizations to provide basic HCBC services as a public benefit, while encouraging for-profit organizations to operate individualized or high-end services with government subsidies.

Currently, HCBC facilities are available in most urban and rural communities. With government bearing personnel and operating costs, community and non-profit organizations hold the advantage in mobilizing a wide range of social resources with volunteers providing elderly care services at minimal cost to users. They can also support and organize mutual support groups among the elderly and residents to offer elderly care services to those needing care—widely practiced currently.

In addition, community and non-profit organizations are also more trusted by the elderly and residents, and can collaborate with family caregivers in providing services. With those needing care mostly over 75 years old having several children as a major source of elderly care services, HCBC administered by community or non-profit organizations can work in partnership with family caregivers. This may contribute to both quality care and lower costs once caregivers have the appropriate skills.

Support Development of Elderly Care Management Tools

Elderly care service management tools such as needs assessments, financing and payment systems, and management information system (MIS) should be developed based on research to prepare for a future when care needs are expected to increase dramatically. Enforcing a nationally standardized needs-assessment mechanism can help government target elderly care resources. The mechanism can screen out those with no need for elderly care services while ensuring those with needs get help. It is particularly important that subsidized elderly care goes to those eligible for the services.

An MIS is essential to effectively operate an elderly care system. A well-designed and implemented MIS can support many important functions: (i) screening, identifying and monitoring care needs of the elderly and their families for proper intervention; (ii) coordinating policies of different government departments and services from different elderly care providers; and (iii) supporting evidence-based policy making in developing the elderly care system.

By collecting and updating data systematically on service inputs, processes, outputs, outcomes and quality, MIS can help the government accumulate experience in improving elderly care policies—such as developing financing and payment mechanisms, improving need assessments, collaborating with private providers, and monitoring needs, services and results.

Strengthen the Role of Street Office/Township Offices

The design and implementation of an effective elderly care system requires collaboration with many government departments—such as civil affairs, finance, health, human resources and social security, education and elderly care providers. "Aging offices" within street offices and townships are in a better position to coordinate stakeholders, and should be strengthened to play a greater role in leading and overseeing implementation of local community-based elderly care systems.

Specifically, these offices should be staffed with workers knowledgeable about aging, elderly care or other related fields, to handle several functions: (i) enforcing and overseeing the implementation of laws and policies relating to the elderly population and elderly care; (ii) planning the local elderly care system and overseeing its operation to ensure proper principles and practices are used; (iii) enforcing standards for services and the workforce; and (iv) providing guidance and support for communities, families and the elderly in operating the elderly care system.

Hand in hand with care for the elderly is the opposite spectrum—ensuring young children get the care they need to develop into vibrant, active citizens.

IMPROVING HUMAN CAPITAL THROUGH EARLY CHILDHOOD DEVELOPMENT

Rural Migration and Left-behind Children

Public services are needed for infant and child health care in poor rural areas; along with isolated caregivers.

How Rural-Urban Migration Increases Vulnerability

Rural-urban migration has created three vulnerable groups: migrant rural workers, landless farmers, and the left-behind population. In 2009, there were roughly 330 million people in these groups: 150 million as the "floating" population (migrant rural workers); 40 million–50 million landless farmers; and 130 million left-behind people.

The massive rural-urban migration that partially fueled the PRC's unprecedented economic expansion also led to many parent-child separations—68.7 million children by 2015. To varying degrees, this protracted separation affected the care, safety, cognitive, social and emotional development of preschool left-behind children. In general, there are no systematic policies for the early development of infants and children aged 0–3 as many lack substantive solutions and public investment.

The establishment of a basic rural public service system began late; with the health care and early education of infants and young children in rural areas not prioritized. Consequently, caregivers had insufficient knowledge of health care or how to

care for infants. Most grassroot rural child health-care workers were part-time village health workers with relatively low education or professional experience. They lacked the awareness, ability and corresponding incentives to provide adequate early childhood development services, leaving them unable to meet the needs of early childhood development (China Development Research Foundation 2017).

The care and education of infants and young children were thus almost entirely undertaken within families, which required their substantial investment in time, energy and money. There were few public health care and educational institutions, and no institutional services from which families could choose.

Since the 1982 abolition of the National Leading Group on Kindergarten Work, there has been no specific government agency overseeing early childhood development. Thus, there is no working mechanism for overall coordination or effective cooperation among relevant departments, resulting in weak policy implementation.

Reforming the Hukou System

In the PRC and many other countries, rural-to-urban migrants are at particular risk. The primary reason in the PRC is the *hukou* (household registration) system, which limits access to critical public services—such as child education, health care, and housing. Steps have been taken to reform the system. But more restrictions need

---

This chapter draws on the background paper prepared by Wei Ha (Ha 2021).

to be lifted. Although reducing *hukou* barriers is necessary, this will not in itself be sufficient for greater inclusion and integration of migrants in urban society—more is needed.

Evidence of the Importance of Early Child Development

Early intervention projects carry high returns and long-term effects; low-cost home visits are particularly important in many developing countries.

Since the mid-20th century, many countries have begun to pay attention to early childhood development, gradually shifting the policy focus to 0–3 year olds. Policy objectives were based on the human capital theory, which argues that human capital development may address the developmental challenges of the poor and promote social equity. Many studies have shown that investing in preventive interventions, such as early childhood development, yields far higher returns and is more effective than investing in remedial interventions, such as remedial education programs and adult education and training. This has long-term implications for enhancing human capital.

History of the Early Childhood Care System

Until the 1990s, while public provisions were given to urban childcare, in rural areas parents had to bear most of the responsibility.

Pre-1990

Under the planned economic system, work units of urban residents assumed most of the functions of social services for children—including meals, education and medical services. Consequently, the responsibility of caring for preschool children was in the units and enterprises where parents worked. In addition to the nurseries and kindergartens[17] organized by units and enterprises, there were also nurseries organized by local women's federations and run by the local governments, which to some extent filled the gap (Zhang 2017). Nurseries and kindergartens run by different entities were financed differently. Those run by government agencies and public institutions received direct fiscal subsidies, whereas those run by public enterprises could deduct these expenses from tax liabilities. Those organized locally raised funds on their own (Cai, Wang, and Zhan 2019). Most nurseries and kindergartens run by state-owned enterprises, governments and public institutions had sufficient funds and quality, while preschool and early education for children outside the system were at a lower level.

In rural areas, during the Great Leap Forward, there were child-care mutual cooperative groups, farm nurseries, year-round day nurseries and other forms of care. Some were spontaneously organized by farmers, while some became part of agricultural producer cooperatives with costs borne by the collective. However, most of the time, rural childcare was mainly through the help of neighbors. In other words, there was a big gap in the supply of preschool education between urban and rural areas and between areas with different economic advantages.

The Regulations on the Administration of Kindergartens promulgated in 1989 stipulated that public kindergartens had to accept children over the age of 3. In doing so, nurseries providing care services for children less than 3 years of age were entirely outside the policy focus (Yue and Xin 2018). It was not until 2010 that early childhood development for children aged 0–3 years was again placed on the policy agenda.

---

[17] Today known as day care centers and preschools.

Mid-1990s to 2010

The number of collective kindergartens decreased significantly during this period; private kindergartens increased rapidly, but there was a policy gap for infants and young children aged 0–3 years.

From the mid-1990s to 2010, kindergartens and nurseries run by enterprises were "closed, suspended, merged and transferred" in a wave of state-owned enterprise reform. Even before that, the financing system of preschool education started to collapse with the abolishment of tax-free status for childcare expenses. As a result, many enterprises stopped or reduced investment in kindergartens and nurseries (Zeng and Xin, 2009). For example, collectively run kindergartens dropped from about 130,000 in 1990 to

about 80,000 in 2000, with their share of total kindergartens falling from 76.2% to 45.9%.

Policy changes led to rapidly decreasing collective kindergartens after 2000, with only 15,000 operating in 2010, or just 0.1 of the total (Figures 10 and 11). At the same time, the state began to encourage social entities to run kindergartens, with a considerable number of enterprise-run kindergartens transformed into private kindergartens. In 1994, the PRC's education statistics yearbook began to include private kindergartens, which numbered 18,300. Afterward, they increased rapidly, reaching 62,200 in 2004, or 52% of kindergartens nationwide. Thus, market forces were driving the supply of preschool education. The number of state preschools rose slowly from 13,000 in 1990 to 44,000 in 2000, before levelling off at 25,000–30,000 a decade later.

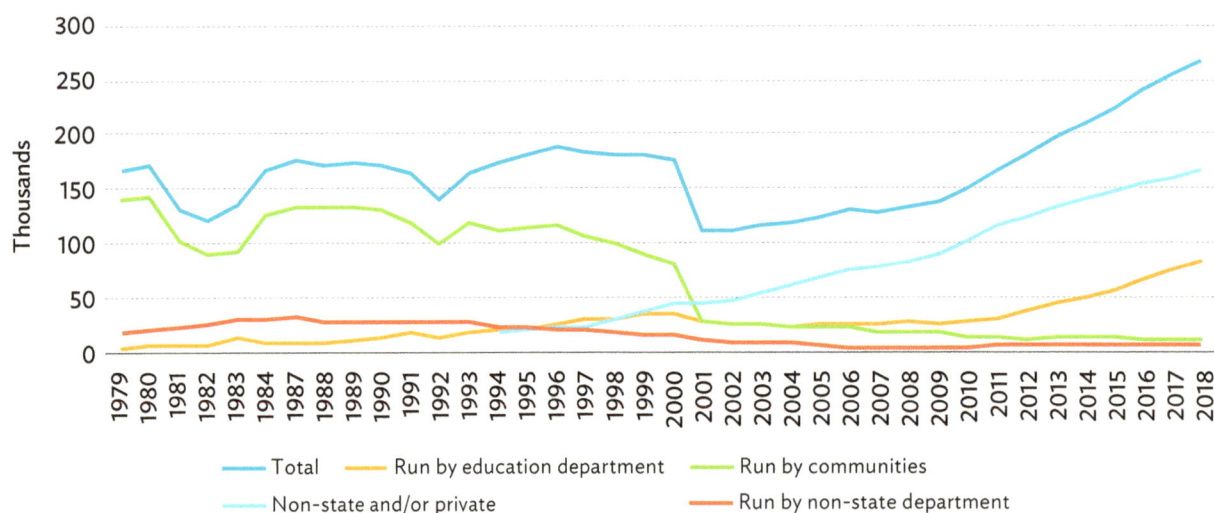

Figure 10: Number of Kindergartens, 1979–2018

Source: China Education Yearbook 1979–2018.

Figure 11: Kindergarten Providers 1979–2018
(% of total)

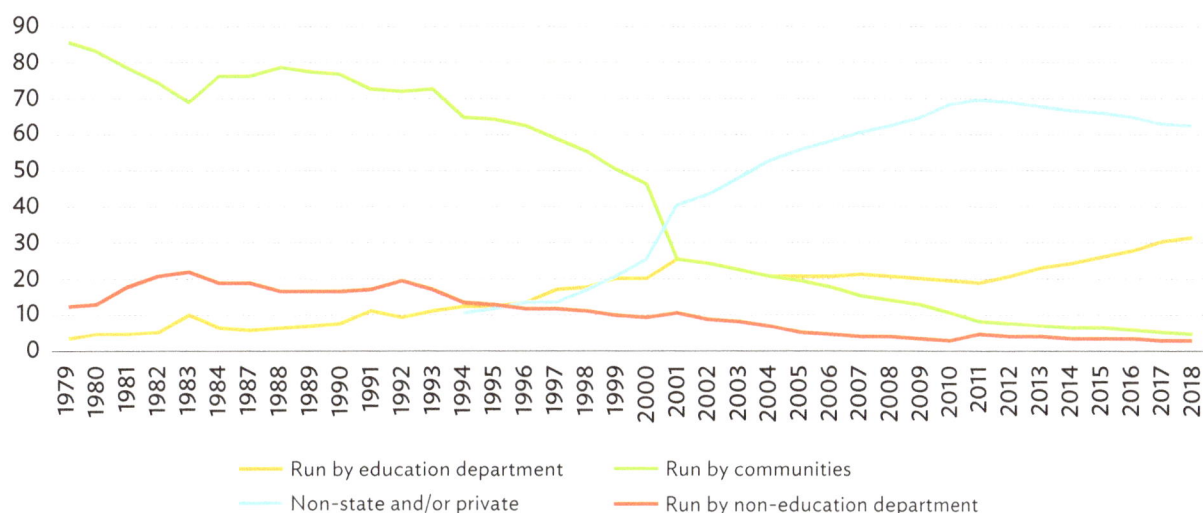

Source: China Education Yearbook 1979–2018.

2010–2020

The government has paid particular attention to early childhood development since the 2012 launch of its 3-year rural action plans.

From 2010 to 2020, private kindergartens continued to proliferate as the government began to increase public investment in preschool education and the number of public kindergartens began to increase. The Outline of the National Plan for Medium and Long Term Education Reform and Development (2010–2020) proposed actively developing preschool education, expanding preschool education resources in various forms, establishing a government-led public and private kindergarten system through social participation, and formulating county-level 3-year action plans for preschool education. It is clear this policy was meant to respond to the longstanding outcry against the affordability and accessibility of preschool education. The transition also benefited from the popularization of compulsory education (those with 9-year compulsory education reached 87.5% by 2010).

By 2020, the PRC has implemented 3-year action plans for preschool education. The financial investment in preschool education nationwide increased from CNY24.4 billion in 2010 to CNY156.4 billion in 2017, a 5.4 times increase. The proportion of preschool education in public educational expenditures was less than 1.5% before 2010, increasing to 4.6% in 2017 (Song 2019) (Figures 12 and 13). By 2018, the gross enrollment rate in the 3 years before school reached 81.7% (Figure 14), and the number of public kindergartens reached about 83,000, or 31% of the total (an increase of 12% over 2011). The number of private kindergartens reached 166,000, or 62% of the total. In February 2020, the Ministry of Education issued its "County Preschool Education Popularization

Inclusive Supervision and Evaluation Measures" to define the main indicators for county preschool education. Main targets included a gross enrollment rate for children aged 3-6 of 85%, with 80% of these children to be served by public preschools (50%) or semi-public preschools (30%). With the completion of the three preschool education action plans, the gross enrollment rate for preschool education was expected to reach 85%.

Figure 12: Public Education Expenditure on Preschool Education, 2000–2017
(CNY billion)

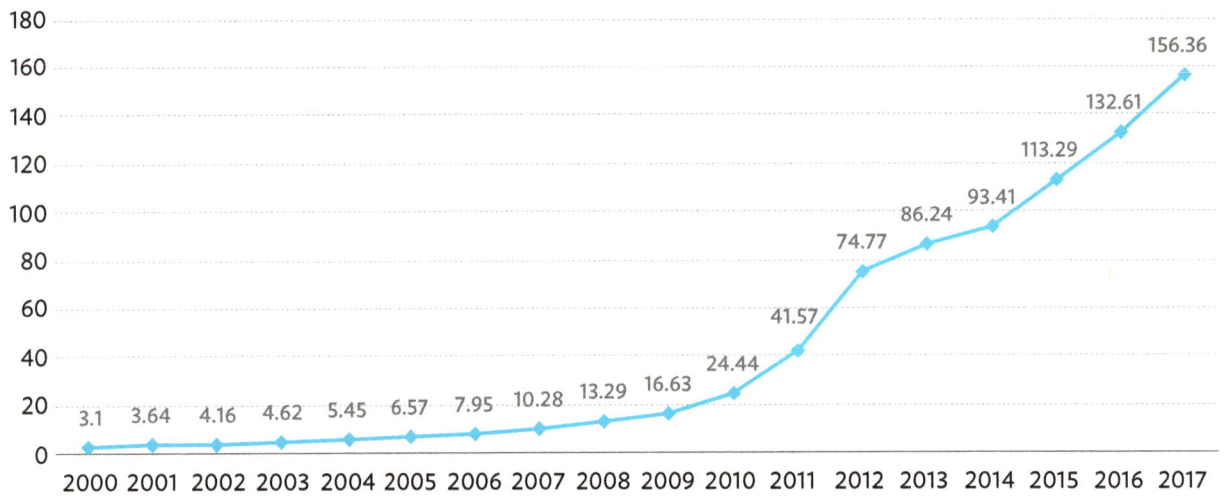

Source: Song, Yingquan. 2019. Contradictions and Reformation of Public Finance in Early Childhood Education and Care in China.

Figure 13: Share of Preschool Education in Total Public Education Expenditures, 2000–2017
(%)

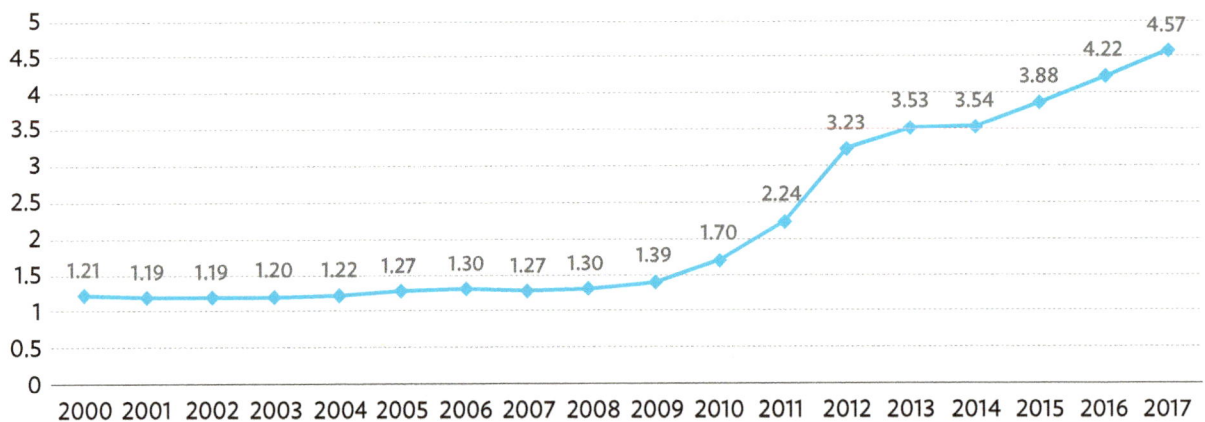

Source: Song, Yingquan. 2019. Contradictions and Reformation of Public Finance in Early Childhood Education and Care in China.

At the same time, the government began to pay particular attention to early childhood development for those aged 0–3 years old. The enrollment rates of preschool children are relatively low, with the enrollment rate across educational institutions in 2017 only 4.1% (Tencent Education 2017). The Outline of the National Plan for Medium- and Long-Term Education Reform and Development (2010–2020) was the first to mention that attention should be paid to the education of infants and young children aged 0–3. In 2012, the Ministry of Education identified pilot cities for early childhood development for infants. The Thirteenth Five-Year Plan for the Development of National Education in 2017 continued to emphasize the development of early education for children aged 0–3.

In April 2018, the State Health and Safety Commission issued an Action Plan for Healthy Children 2018–2020, proposing the implementation of early childhood development activities, promoting the equalization of early childhood development, and promoting early childhood development services in rural areas, communities and families. Shortly afterward, the State Council issued its *"2019 Guiding*

Opinions on Promoting the Development of Infant Care Services under the age of 3", setting out the principle of "family-oriented, complementary care", strengthening support for families and communities, increasing support for infant care services in rural and poor areas, and delineating the division of responsibilities among government departments. Provincial governments issued corresponding implementation opinions to promote the development of infant care services according to State Council requirements.

Between 2011 and 2016, the central government invested around CNY100 billion in early childhood development (or 0.7% of total public investment), with CNY360 billion in additional investment coming from local governments (0.5% of total local government public investment). This was significantly above the CNY24.4 billion invested in 2010. Enrollment rates for 3-6 year olds in preschools have risen sharply and is on track to reach the 85% target. Despite the fiscal challenges due to the COVID-19 pandemic, the central government remains committed to prioritize intergovernmental transfers for early childhood development in the 2020 budget.

Figure 14: Gross Preschool Enrollment Rate, 2009–2020
(%)

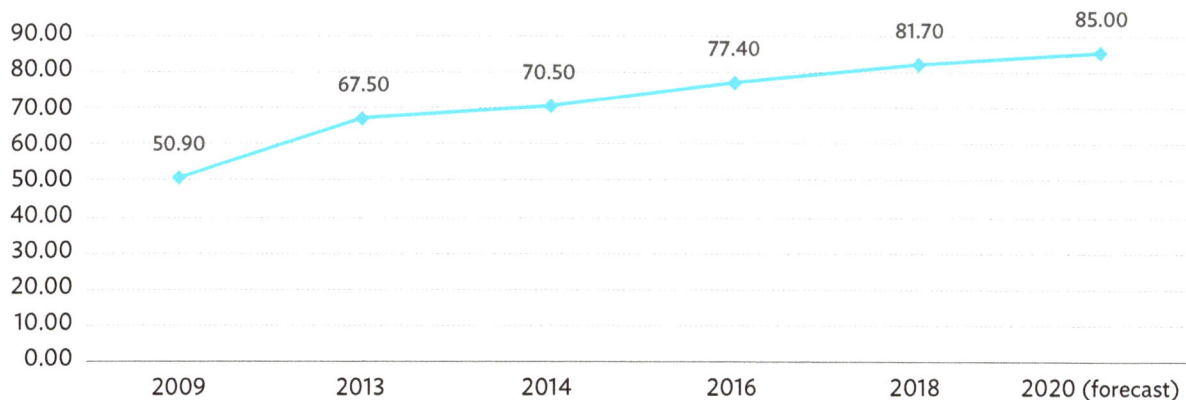

Source: Ministry of Education Information Aggregate.

Key Policy Recommendations

One important way to reduce poverty is to improve the quality of human capital in poor rural areas; investing in early childhood development has the highest returns.

In 2020, the basic requirements for rural poverty alleviation include the supply of adequate food and clothing, effective compulsory education, basic medical care and housing. This "new normal" will shift the PRC's economic growth away from relying mainly on manufacturing to relying more on technological progress and innovation.

One key to this transformation is to improve the quality of future human capital. Early childhood development is an important focus for a national health, education and poverty alleviation strategy. The current strategy should prioritize preschool children in poor rural areas, using comprehensive and holistic interventions in nutrition, health, parenting and education to ensure children in poor rural areas are given equal opportunities for early development. It is important to accelerate the formulation and implementation of policies for the early development of infants and young children aged 0–3 in poor rural areas.

Early childhood development policies need to be more comprehensive and equitable, with a focus on rural poor children.

In 2019, the State Council issued the "*Guiding Opinions on Promoting the Development of Infant Care Services under the Age of 3.*" Early education for infants aged 0–3 has gradually received more attention, with relevant implementation guidelines issued. While expanding public investment is essential, narrowing the gap in coverage and quality of services between urban and rural areas is also being considered.

Learning from the successful Head Start Program in the United States, there is increased focus on early education for children from low-income families. The aim is to gradually expand the scope of services equitably. There is a particular need for expanding financial aid for vulnerable groups of children, who account for about 10% of kindergarten children (Song 2019). There is "rural depression" in preschool education funding (Liu 2019). Therefore, the early development policy for infants and young children aged 0–3 should avoid repeating the unfair financial distribution of preschool education. Financial support should discard the "public-only" limitation for funding. This means offering aid on a standardized basis to all institutions, regardless of whether they are run by government departments, enterprises, universities, collectives, or by social organizations and nongovernmental organizations. So long as they provide inclusive education, financial support should be available to better leverage additional support (Lijuan et al. 2019).

Early childhood development policies should provide multifaceted support for caregivers.

Infants in poor rural areas face developmental lags in nutrition, health, cognition, language, along with social and emotional barriers. These correlate with those of caregivers. They are an essential part of rural public health care and medical services. They should be capable of providing physical examinations for young children's psychological and behavioral development, as well as offer breastfeeding guidance, supplementary food provision, reasonable dietary assistance and other services.

It is also essential to help parents establish awareness of early childhood development, popularize scientific knowledge of parenting, and correct poor parenting. Enhancing knowledge about child nutrition and creating an excellent nurturing environment will help promote their cognitive, linguistic, social and emotional development.

An essential part of the Head Start program was the inclusion of parents in implementation, including helping parents set goals for family cooperation, participation in maternal education and child development, participation in child nutrition and mental health services, and participation in community services and home visiting services (Tong and Nie 2008). The concept of "parental participation" should be incorporated into early childhood development policies to provide support for caregivers, especially those teaching and interacting with children to improve the family environment.

Provide flexible and diverse early childhood development services, drawing on the PRC's past and international experience.

Early childhood development services should account for actual family situations, the level of local economic development, and provide a flexible and diverse menu of services. Drawing lessons from its rich experience during the 1950s and 1970s, the PRC should adopt full-time, part-time, half-day, hourly, night care and other forms of care to meet the diverse and multifaceted needs of parents for the education and care for children aged 0–3 (Lijuan et al. 2019). This should include full-time services, mainly for families with two working parents and a lack of intergenerational

support; day care services in the form of "monthly care"; "half-monthly care" and "weekly care" should be provided as well as half-day services—mainly for part-time working mothers or families with some intergenerational support.

It is important to note that a significant number of poverty-stricken rural areas are located in remote and mountainous areas, with inconvenient transportation. Thus, many institutional services cannot reach the village level. This can be addressed with the help of home visits, which requires both adequate finance and personnel to support rural communities as they expand the scope of public services for early childhood development.

To cater to these needs, institutions can offer morning or afternoon care for parents to choose accordingly. For example, they could offer temporary services to meet short-term educational and care needs of families with special work responsibilities—such as short-time care, weekend care and holiday care. In addition to relying on early childhood development services provided by educational institutions, families themselves can also serve as units of early childhood development. Taking the "Head Start Program" as an example, its standard service model was to let children receive education in Child Development Centers. However, there was an additional family service model to assist parents educate children and improve the quality of family education.

7 RESPONSE TO THE COVID-19 PANDEMIC AND HEALTH SYSTEM REFORM

Experience in Responding to Epidemics and the COVID-19 Pandemic

Investments in health included reforms which resulted in near universal health insurance coverage; nonetheless, the PRC is determined to use infrastructure and technology to incorporate lessons learned from the recent pandemic.

Emerging Infectious Diseases

In 2003, the world was confronted with the emergence of a new infectious disease—severe acute respiratory syndrome (SARS). At that time, there was no functioning infectious disease surveillance system, and an outdated reporting system slowed data collection and delayed responses. Since then, the government has made substantial investments to improve infrastructure, surveillance systems, and emergency preparedness and response capacity. It developed a real-time monitoring system that is now a model for surveillance and infectious disease response.[18]

The origin of SARS was never confirmed, but coronavirus has been isolated from palm civets, raccoon dogs, ferret badgers, cats, and bats, which might serve as animal reservoirs or infection sources for humans.[19]

Avian influenza (H5N1) was first identified in Guangdong in 1996. The disease is found in poultry, including chickens, ducks, and geese.[20] Confirmed human cases were identified in the PRC between 2005 and 2011. In March 2013, the avian influenza H7N9 virus was identified in Anhui Province and Shanghai City.[21] It is spread by direct contact with infected birds or indirect contact with virus contaminants, with humans mainly infected by contact with infected chickens. Wild birds play an important role as long-distance animal reservoirs of the virus.[22]

In December 2019, the PRC reported to the World Health Organization (WHO) cases of pneumonia of unknown cause occurring in Wuhan, Hubei Province.[23] Initial patients exhibited clinical symptoms resembling viral pneumonia. The country's capacity to detect cases allowed

This chapter draws on the background paper prepared by Najibullah Habib.

---

18 Wang L, Wang Y, Jin S, et al. Emergence and control of infectious diseases in China. Lancet 2008;372(9649):1598-605.
19 Shi Z, Hu Z. A review of studies on animal reservoirs of the SARS coronavirus. Virus Res 2008;133: 74–87.
20 Martin V, Pfeiffer DU, Zhou X, Xiao X, Prosser DJ, Guo F, et al. Spatial distribution and risk factors of highly pathogenic avian influenza (HPAI) H5N1 in China. PLoS Pathog 2011;7: e1001308.
21 Gao R, Cao B, Hu Y, Feng Z, Wang D, Hu W, et al. Human infection with a novel avian-origin influenza A (H7N9) virus. N Engl J Med 2013; 368:1888–97.
22 Prosser DJ, Cui P, Takekawa JY, Tang M, Hou Y, Collins BM, et al. Wild bird migration across the Qinghai-Tibetan plateau: a transmission route for highly pathogenic H5N1. PLoS One 2011;6: e17622.
23 WHO. Novel coronavirus (2019-NCoV) situation report 1. Geneva: World Health Organization, 11 January 2020.

for the early recognition and verification of the pathogen. Viral genetic sequencing of samples indicated a novel coronavirus.[24] It was named the 2019 novel coronavirus (COVID-19) and confirmed to have 75%-80% resemblance to SARS-CoV.2. On 11 March 2020, the WHO Director General declared COVID-19 a pandemic.

Improving Preparedness and Response

The COVID-19 pandemic, along with previous infectious diseases, revealed the strengths and weaknesses of the PRC's health system.

Incorporating the hard lessons from the 2003 SARS outbreak, the government invested heavily in disease control and prevention and has lowered the damage caused by infectious diseases. It earmarked CNY6.8 billion ($850 million) for disease control and prevention, CNY2 billion ($250 million) to upgrade county hospitals and purchase medical facilities; and CNY7 billion ($875 million) from local governments. This improved public health infrastructure with new laboratories, upgraded surveillance systems, and increased the number of qualified public health professionals.[25]

The government allocated CNY19.3 billion to medical institutions across the country for COVID-19 to ease the pressure of out-of-pocket medical payments. At least CNY3.7 billion went to hard-hit Hubei Province.[26]

After SARS, the government enacted a series of laws and regulations to prevent and control infectious diseases in humans, domestic animals, and wild animals. These included the Infectious Diseases Prevention Law, Emergency Regulations on Public Health Emergencies, Major Animal Disease Emergency Ordinance, Animal Epidemic Prevention Law, National Sudden Major Animal Disease Contingency Plans, Terrestrial Wild Animal Epidemic Sources and Disease Monitoring Standards.[27]

These helped generate preparedness and response initiatives that resulted in quick COVID-19 intervention. The PRC took extraordinary public health measures in response to COVID-19, moving swiftly and decisively to ensure early case identification, prompt laboratory testing, facility-based isolation, contact-tracing, and quarantines.[28] At the community level, social distancing was implemented on a grand scale. There has been stark improvement in reporting SARS and COVID-19 infections (Figure 15).

The COVID-19 pandemic is a compelling reason to continue building health security and prioritizing funding for health infrastructure, including data and logistics management. The PRC is a pioneer in technological innovation. And it is important to build on this to support preparedness and response mechanisms, for example, in mapping those potentially affected , and for follow-up and monitoring.

24 Zhu N, Zhang D, Wang W, et al. A novel coronavirus from patients with pneumonia in China, 2019. *N Engl J Med* 2020; 382: 727–33.
25 SARS Epidemic and its aftermath in China: A Political Perspective https://www.ncbi.nlm.nih.gov/books/NBK92479/.
26 https://www.globaltimes.cn/content/1184060.shtml.
27 Wang CJ, Xiang H, Liu DR, He JJ, Nie SF. Reflection on legal construction of Chinese public health emergencies. Med Soc 2007; 20:38–40.
28 Wilder-Smith A, Freedman DO. Isolation, quarantine, social distancing and community containment: pivotal role for old-style public health measures in the novel coronavirus (2019-nCoV) outbreak. *J Travel Med* 2020; 27: taaa020.

Figure 15: SARS and COVID-19 in the People's Republic of China

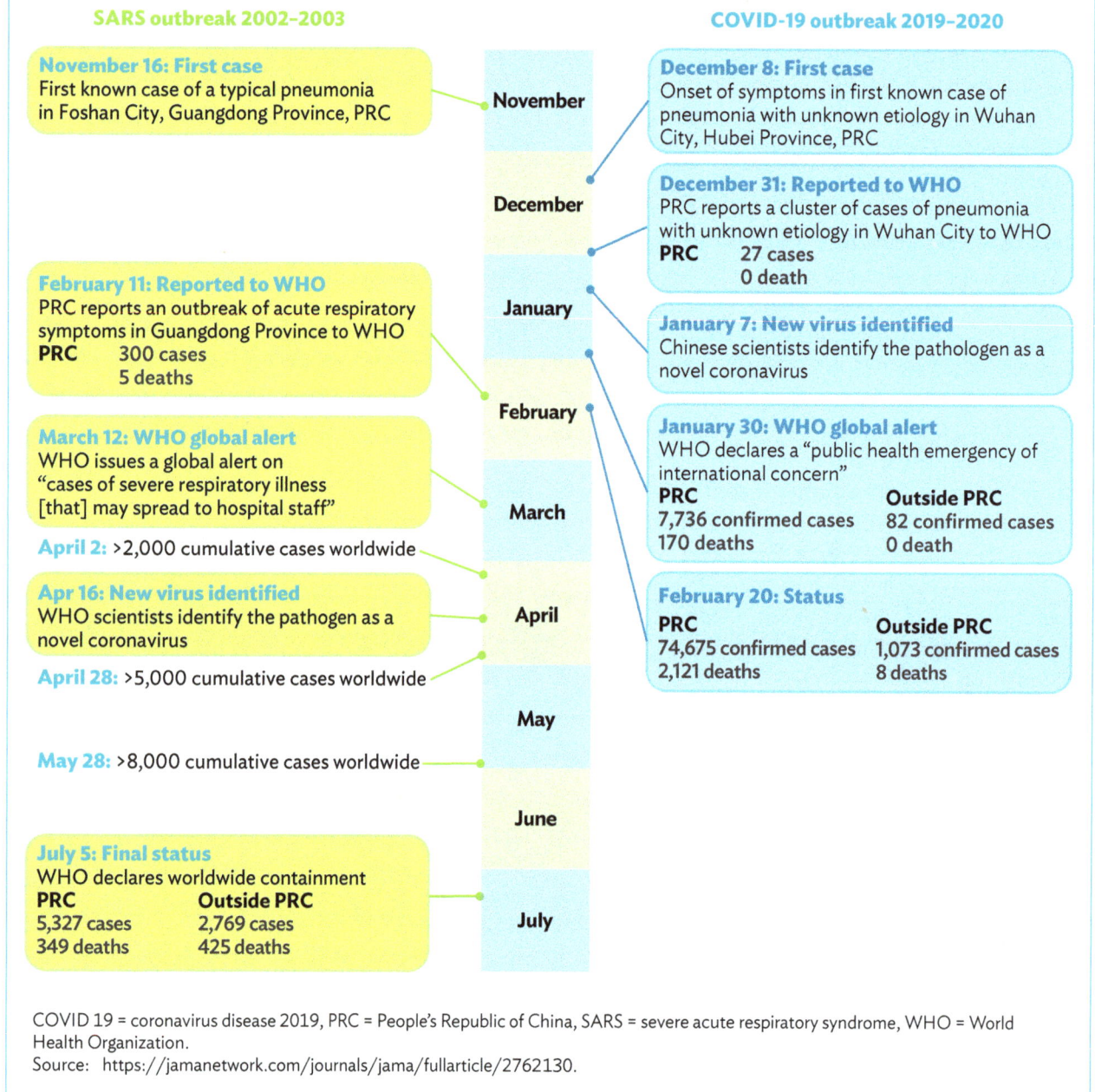

SARS outbreak 2002–2003

COVID-19 outbreak 2019–2020

November 16: First case
First known case of a typical pneumonia in Foshan City, Guangdong Province, PRC

December 8: First case
Onset of symptoms in first known case of pneumonia with unknown etiology in Wuhan City, Hubei Province, PRC

December 31: Reported to WHO
PRC reports a cluster of cases of pneumonia with unknown etiology in Wuhan City to WHO
PRC   27 cases
            0 death

February 11: Reported to WHO
PRC reports an outbreak of acute respiratory symptoms in Guangdong Province to WHO
PRC   300 cases
            5 deaths

January 7: New virus identified
Chinese scientists identify the pathologen as a novel coronavirus

March 12: WHO global alert
WHO issues a global alert on "cases of severe respiratory illness [that] may spread to hospital staff"

January 30: WHO global alert
WHO declares a "public health emergency of international concern"
PRC	**Outside PRC**
7,736 confirmed cases	82 confirmed cases
170 deaths	0 death

April 2: >2,000 cumulative cases worldwide

Apr 16: New virus identified
WHO scientists identify the pathogen as a novel coronavirus

February 20: Status
PRC	**Outside PRC**
74,675 confirmed cases	1,073 confirmed cases
2,121 deaths	8 deaths

April 28: >5,000 cumulative cases worldwide

May 28: >8,000 cumulative cases worldwide

July 5: Final status
WHO declares worldwide containment
PRC	**Outside PRC**
5,327 cases	2,769 cases
349 deaths	425 deaths

Timeline months (center): November, December, January, February, March, April, May, June, July

COVID 19 = coronavirus disease 2019, PRC = People's Republic of China, SARS = severe acute respiratory syndrome, WHO = World Health Organization.
Source: https://jamanetwork.com/journals/jama/fullarticle/2762130.

Framework for Pandemic Preparedness and Health Security

Adequate health security means being prepared for any public health threat, including rapidly spreading disease outbreaks. Constant mutation and adaptation are the survival mechanisms of microbes. The outbreaks of SARS, Avian influenza and COVID-19 show how changes in the way humanity inhabits the planet have given microbes new opportunities to spread. These include rapid, unplanned urbanization that crowds people together (sometimes without water supply or sanitation), the close proximity of animals (including chickens and pigs), incursions into previously uninhabited forests, industrialized food production, and the remarkable increase in international travel and trade. Climate change and unusual weather patterns affect the distribution of wild animals and new diseases.

Preparing for a pandemic and strengthening health security require a high degree of coordination between ministries and agencies, and the financial and technical support of the international community. Having experienced many outbreaks from emerging infectious diseases, the PRC can lead the development of surveillance and response systems that could serve as an example for other developing countries.

The potential agenda for long-term health security includes implementing International Health Regulations (IHR 2005)[29] and the Asia Pacific Strategy for Emerging Diseases and Public Health Emergencies (APSED 2017).[30] IHR provides the legal charter for the collective responsibility of countries, WHO and other intergovernmental organizations for global health security. APSED was first developed in 2005 as a common framework for the Asia and Pacific region to address shared threats as mandated by the IHR. APSED was updated in 2010 and 2017, with the latest version emphasizing the strengthening of health systems and capacities for greater health security, using an all-hazards approach in recognition of novel infections, antimicrobial resistance, unsafe food and water, natural disasters, chemical and radiological emergencies and other public health emergencies.

Private Sector and Health Security

Sustainable health security will require getting more stakeholders involved in embracing a wider range of private sector partners. The leading

drivers of new human disease are activities such as land use change, new food production systems, and trade and travel. This highlights the valuable role the private sector can play in boosting health security.

The private sector continues to evolve and stepped up initiatives during the pandemic. Some provided direct donations or in-kind support. They use their resources for the benefit of affected communities and developed new products and services to address unmet needs.

Digital technology in the COVID-19 response included the widespread use of mobile apps for medical information and services. Expanding their functionality and the use of social media apps was an important way forward for outbreak response. It showed the importance of the private sector in developing valuable new media during crises.

Governments need to work with the private sector to avoid disrupting medical supply due to an epidemic, including protective equipment, and medical devices and other life-saving products. Moreover, the government must encourage development of new vaccines, diagnostics, and therapeutics at the onset of new, unknown outbreaks. Arrangements must be in place before outbreaks to capitalize on the added value of private sector preparation and response programs.

Corporations are an important backbone of the PRC economy. To function, they need healthy employees. They need to keep their supply chains operating smoothly. And they need to communicate effectively with both partners and customers. Thus, to limit disruption, it makes sense to work with public health authorities to prepare for and plan responses to any threat. It is a valuable investment to avoid lost productivity

---

29   World Health Organization, International Health Regulation (2005). https://www.who.int/ihr/publications/9789241580496/en/.
30   World Health Organization. 2017. Asia Pacific Strategy for Emerging Diseases and Public Health Emergencies.

and sales, reduce potential human suffering—and health-care claims. Corporations and the government need to define their responsibilities during outbreaks.

Vulnerable Population Groups

The sudden stop of economic activity and workforce flow in the aftermath of the COVID-19 pandemic will greatly impact poor and vulnerable groups: childless seniors, orphans, the disabled, the unemployed, and rural migrants, among others.

A person or a population group not considered vulnerable at the outset of an outbreak can become vulnerable depending on the outbreak response. For instance, extreme quarantines can result in the sudden loss of income or access to social support. Moreover, in times of outbreaks or pandemics, identifying those who might become vulnerable is a challenge. In the case of COVID-19, those with existing health conditions and those in certain socioeconomic groups will potentially struggle to cope financially, mentally and physically.

PRC officials provided extensive support to vulnerable groups during the pandemic.

A series of responses were enacted by the State Council to support vulnerable groups since mid-February (Table 5). It included doubling social assistance and monthly subsidies from March to June 2020 to cover for 8 million people, mainly the jobless and orphans. To date, the government has extended assistance to more than 67 million people. Announced expenditures to help vulnerable groups during the first 4 months of 2020 was CNY156 billion, about 6% more than the total spent in 2019.

Continuing Poverty Alleviation Goals in Light of the Pandemic

In the aftermath of the pandemic, special attention was given to preventing vulnerable groups from slipping into short- or medium-term poverty.

The central government invested CNY126.1 billion ($18.1 billion) in 2019 on its anti-poverty campaign, targeting in particular rural areas where

Table 5: Summary of Benefits to Assist Vulnerable Groups during COVID-19

Implementing Ministries	Coverage	Amount/Number of Beneficiaries
Ministry of Civil Affairs	Price subsidies to support low-income people	CNY1.9 billion handed to more than 61 million disadvantaged people throughout the PRC In Hubei, 3.7 million people received CNY440 million
Ministry of Human Resources and Social Security	Unemployment benefits	CNY93 billion distributed to 2.3 million jobless people as of the end of March 2020
Ministry of Human Resources and Social Security	One-time temporary living allowances for migrant workers	CNY410 million to 670,000 people In Wuhan, stranded workers in the city received CNY3,000 in cash as an emergency allowance
National Development and Reform Commission	Temporary monthly social benefits/subsidies that are linked to inflation	CNY16.5 billion to cover 8 million people
Ministry of Human Resources and Social Security	Additional health insurance	CNY2 billion
Total allocated for vulnerable groups		Approvals in January–April 2020 = CNY156 billion Full year 2019 = CNY147.2 billion 6.0% increase

COVID-19 = coronavirus disease 2019, CNY = Chinese yuan, PRC = People's Republic of China.
Source: State Council. 2020a. More subsidies soon for at-risk groups. http://english.www.gov.cn/statecouncil/ministries/202004/11/content_WS5e91252bc6d0c201c2cc0abe.html (accessed 28 August 2020).

more than 564 million people live. The government announced on 21 November 2020 that efforts to eliminate absolute poverty in 2020 were complete, removing the last 52 counties previously considered poor. This last group covered some 5.5 million people at the end of 2019, down from the 99.0 million at the end of 2012 who were below the poverty threshold.

However, with COVID-19 and the loss of income among vulnerable groups, there were spikes in poverty, missed meals for children, and reduced access to health care far beyond COVID-19 (Evans and Over 2020). This is particularly true in rural areas where most smallholders reside and work. Marchioso (2020) believes that, due to the lack of income during lockdown, many poor households might have sold assets and spent their meager savings to deal with the impact, making them more vulnerable to poverty than before.

To sustain poverty alleviation gains and counteract the impact of COVID-19, the State Council Leading Group Office of Poverty Alleviation and Development and Ministry of Finance issued a joint circular on 25 February 2020, that regions impacted by COVID-19 will be given funding support (Zhao 2020). This policy directed local or county governments to use the funds to support industrial projects, promote employment, and secure livelihoods for the poor and migrant workers. The circular also stressed filling temporary jobs in sanitation, disinfection, epidemic prevention and inspection, while subsidies for transportation, living expenses and others were also encouraged. At a press briefing on 12 March 2020, the poverty alleviation office highlighted the need for poverty-alleviation projects to be dynamically adjusted in a timely manner to counteract the impact of the epidemic (State Council 2020c).

A major short-term challenge for the PRC is to ensure that those who became more vulnerable due to the pandemic—from lost income, reduced savings and asset sales—do not slip back into poverty. Fortunately, this is precisely what the government is trying to do.

Key Policy Recommendations

A comprehensive set of policies is needed to strengthen the PRC's response to future pandemics.

Further Reforming the Health System

The PRC may have a strong public health system, but capacity still needs to increase to avoid the risk of excessive demand over a sustained period. This requires an extensive response with strong support from the international community. The government should design longer-term policies that boost prevention—depending on how prepared the health system is and the level of the population's vulnerability. Differentiated preparedness and response may be considered to ensure optimal support to the most vulnerable areas and population groups.

Climate change can intensify emerging and reemerging infectious diseases threats. Priority should be given to a scientific study that will include ecological factors, climate, and social and human behavior.

As the PRC grapples with existing and potentially new infectious diseases, it must address the challenges and weaknesses of current control efforts. There is a need to motivate and provide sufficient incentives to public health frontline workers to undertake disease control. Retooling or updating skills on outbreak control and prevention is necessary. Substantial time and effort will be needed to train those who further control existing and new infectious diseases.

Hospitals should be part of a network that prevents and, if needed, controls the outbreak of infectious diseases. Staff need to be better trained and motivated to properly diagnose, report, and manage any outbreak.

There is plenty of room for innovative technological development for the "One Health" approach and other aspects of emerging infectious diseases preparedness. It will help the health security program use technology to map potential vulnerable groups, their exact location and magnitude of risk, and impact on certain population groups. Response can be improved with technology that enables better logistics management during outbreaks.

Economic Policies in Response to the Pandemic

The pandemic showed that short-term policies are also needed to help rural migrants cope with economic shocks.

Unemployment benefits can be distributed to unemployed migrants to build rural roads, telecommunications, irrigation, and other productive assets. Part of the package could also be used to help returned migrants start new businesses in order to regenerate rural economic activity and employment. Because migrants predominately work for micro- and small enterprises, government financial and policy support to small and medium-sized enterprises can help mitigate adverse income effects.

Longer-term measures should focus on revitalizing the rural sector and strengthening rural-urban linkages.

Productive sectors must be revitalized— including agriculture and food and their post-production rural value chains. The PRC already plans to prioritize agriculture and

rural development and advance a pipeline of major projects to facilitate production and consumption (according to guidelines jointly issued by seven departments, including the Ministry of Agriculture and Rural Affairs). Rural education, health and nutrition, particularly for children and women, must be re-emphasized or prioritized. Future human capital including education and health is a foundation for alleviating poverty, improving the well-being of the rural population and long-term rural modernization.

To make migrants, smallholder farmers, the urban poor and other vulnerable groups more resilient, the social security system should be integrated. It should cover both rural and urban populations. These safety nets, which include unemployment insurance, can be cash or in-kind transfers, depending upon the local context. And they should be accompanied by interventions by health and nutrition officials. These investments can lower mortality rates of infectious diseases, as nutrition levels and mortality rates are intricately interlinked. Social safety nets are also crucial to recovery in post-epidemic or pandemic periods.

Strengthening rural-urban linkages are crucial for revitalizing rural areas and ending poverty in both rural and urban areas. These include physical, economic, social, and political links. Urbanization increases food demand and changes diets. New demand can create opportunities for rural producers to improve their livelihoods. Broken value chains and poor coordination weaken these links, hampering progress in nutrition and food security. New rural infrastructure investments in connecting roads, electricity, storage, communication and information, among others—in both local communities and intermediate towns—can build hubs of economic activity benefiting both rural smallholders and urban centers.

The issues of rapid aging, urbanization, and population density make the country relatively more susceptible to both the spread and impact of disease.

The challenges of an increasingly aging and rapidly urbanizing population need to be considered in making cities healthier. These include improving health infrastructure and the accessibility of health-care services. Well-integrated urban planning includes distributed and decentralized urban health services, early detection of infectious diseases, and measures for vulnerable groups such as the elderly.

Urban health investments can effectively and efficiently benefit a growing urban and aging population. Cities must therefore holistically govern, plan, and invest to promote public and community health, healthy lifestyles, gender and age equality, disease prevention, and improved social services. This needs to be integrated within universal urban design to ensure that public spaces, sidewalks, parks, and buildings are accessible to people of all ages and the physically impaired. Cities need to integrate an age-friendly public transport system with safe and convenient sidewalks, bicycle parking, parks, public spaces, and public service facilities (Box 5). The much-needed low-carbon climate-resilient urban planning and design will also contribute to improved health—for example, benefits from reduced emissions and risk of climate-related disasters such as flooding, droughts, heat waves, and storm surges.

Box 5: Making Cities Age-Friendly

The combination of rapid urbanization and aging in the People's Republic of China (PRC)—among other countries—is creating an urban society with four generations living under the same roof. This profound transformation is persuading urban planners and decision-makers to integrate the management of health and social needs of densely populated and aging cities into urban planning, along with the other urgent issues of climate change and the environment. A healthy and age-friendly city promotes equality, good governance, well-being, innovation, and knowledge sharing. It provides for active mobility, food production, gardening, availability of sports arenas, and ways of social exchange. An age-friendly city enhances quality of life by anticipating and responding flexibly to the needs and preferences of the elderly, as well as children and other vulnerable groups like the physically impaired. The Asian Development Bank (ADB) has published several documents to help guide urban planners in integrating sustainable health care and age-friendly systems into urban planning and management. The two-stage holistic and evidence-based framework uses two tools: a Health Impact Assessment and guide for Healthy and Age-Friendly City Action and Management Planning. The framework incorporates lessons and best practices from ADB projects in the PRC.

Sources: https://events.development.asia/learning-events/healthy-and-age-friendly-cities-peoples-republic-china.
https://development.asia/explainer/how-develop-healthy-and-age-friendly-city.

8 CONCLUDING REMARKS — ADDRESSING VULNERABILITY AND FISCAL SUSTAINABILITY

The PRC has a long and successful record of poverty reduction and alleviation. This came as a result of sustained rapid economic growth and a strong commitment to anti-poverty policies. When reforms began in the late 1970s, more than 80% of the population lived in absolute poverty (see footnote 1). In February 2021, the government officially announced it had eradicated absolute poverty.

Thus, the PRC's new poverty strategy will (i) treat poverty as multidimensional; (ii) reinvigorate rural development; (iii) develop an integrated rural-urban poverty strategy; and (iv) address vulnerability to poverty. This report deals mainly with vulnerability.

Vulnerability refers to the likelihood that—at some time in the future—an individual or household will experience a level of well-being that falls below a socially acceptable benchmark. Ensuring growth is inclusive creates new economic opportunities and makes them available to all segments of society. Thus, inclusivity and vulnerability are inversely related. If development becomes more inclusive, it reduces the size of the vulnerable population. Four specific vulnerable groups are targeted in this report: (i) the vulnerable elderly; (ii) young children of rural migrants; (iii) the rural population and rural-to-urban migrants; and (iv) those whose access to health care is jeopardized by urbanization and aging. The choice of groups is largely based on the main demographic drivers of structural transformation—an aging society and urbanization.

Balancing economic growth with social and macroeconomic stability was one of the critical factors that led to the PRC's success. The government applied a mix of fiscal, administrative, and employment policies designed to maintain social stability during this 40-year period of rapid economic and structural change. In particular, anti-poverty policies were clearly reflected in government spending priorities. As the PRC continues to modernize its economy, the same vision, core values, and guiding principles should be followed to ensure that social policy reform leads to inclusive development. An important question raised in this report is how much fiscal support is needed to finance social services and protection, and how much of the burden should be shouldered by individuals and households. The government must be circumspect over the role it must play. After averaging 1.3% of GDP from 1990–2014, the government budget deficit jumped to an average 4.0% during 2015–2019, reaching 4.9% in 2019. The PRC needs to strike the appropriate balance between its own capabilities and the availability of other resources. It needs to avoid the predicament faced by many advanced countries—a fiscal crisis arising in part from unsustainable entitlement programs.

To address both vulnerability and fiscal sustainability, this report explores policies that improve the quality of life of vulnerable groups but do not necessarily require fiscal support. There might also be a need to alter the composition of government expenditures—to meet evolving strategic priorities while maintaining fiscal sustainability. This will require fiscal discipline as well as budgetary procedures that allow resource reallocation over time from lower- to higher priority government programs. Another set of policy measures deals with issues of efficiency— to improve the effectiveness and coverage of spending programs without the need for additional government resources. In some cases, this will require private sector participation.

This report discusses four ways the PRC can reform its fiscal system to ensure fiscal sustainability while at the same time reduce vulnerability: (i) contain government expenditures as a share of GDP but change their composition to align with new challenges—such as higher allocations for social and environmental public investment and recurrent expenditures; (ii) improve the efficiency of revenue mobilization, for example, by changing revenue structures; (iii) reform intergovernmental fiscal relations by better aligning available resources with expenditure responsibility at different levels of government; and (iv) strengthen the management of government finances and improve the efficiency of public expenditures. This report focuses on the first and third aspects.

Case studies from three provinces—Guangdong, Hunan, and Yunnan—provide useful insights. The Guangdong case study focuses on measures that can enhance the efficacy and efficiency of spending programs. The Hunan case study describes how spending programs are directed at specific vulnerable groups. And the case study of Yongsheng County, in Yunnan Province, describes general measures to improve efficacy and efficiency as well as specific programs that address poverty and vulnerability.

There are many examples in the report of public goods or government interventions consistent with the criteria described above. They are designed to reduce poverty and vulnerability. However, their impact on fiscal space depends on the structure of the overall policy program.

1. Promoting rural land rights can increase agricultural productivity.
2. Direct subsidies to grain farmers, to buy new seed varieties, and to use agricultural machinery can boost farm income and reduce rural-urban income gaps.
3. Modern agricultural infrastructure for small-scale (or water-saving) irrigation, reservoir reinforcement, soil improvement, mechanization, and ecological protection can increase productivity. Later, government support for rural roads and transport, telecommunications, electricity and energy supply promotes better market access.
4. Rural environmental infrastructure requires more investment, for waste management, landscape and ecotourism facilities. The public and private sectors can work together to better use underutilized rural resources—including organic waste and by products to generate economic activity and improve environmental management.
5. Recent institutional frameworks and policies were designed to improve the agricultural and rural environment. These include protecting and rehabilitating agricultural land resources, regulating the use of chemical fertilizers, pesticides and other chemicals, and protecting agricultural water resources.
6. The PRC's "No. 1 central document" for 2008 called for higher rural public service provisions in rural education, basic medical services, family planning, rural culture, transportation, and rural utilities. These are currently offered through three main social security nets: the social assistance system; a new rural cooperative medical care system; and a new rural social pension insurance system.

7. The digital transformation affects rural development through e-commerce— it provides a new model of development led by the private sector.
8. A rural minimum living security system uses targeted cash transfers for those with an annual net per capita income below local minimum living standards.
9. Private sector involvement in elderly care has been encouraged through preferential policies such as free land allocation, exemption of taxes and fees, lower utility costs, and promoting public-private partnerships by contracting out public residential care facilities for private operation.
10. The government also provides policy and financial support for rural migrants.

The response to the COVID-19 pandemic will spawn a new normal—under which the vulnerability of certain groups is enhanced, or new vulnerable groups created. The government's early response may hint at future programs and reforms. For example, there is a need for sufficient incentives for public health frontline workers to practice disease control. Retooling or updating skills on outbreak control and prevention is necessary. Hospital staff need to be better trained and motivated to properly diagnose, report, and manage infectious diseases. And hospitals should become part of a network that controls and prevents the outbreak of future infectious diseases.

Many actions are also directed toward vulnerable groups. The pandemic led to several immediate economic measures, such as substantial assistance for the hardest hit rural migrants. But medium- to long-term policies should remain focused on revitalizing the rural sector and strengthening rural-urban linkages. For example, an integrated rural and urban social security system, including unemployment insurance, is a more sustainable solution to build resilience among migrants, smallholder farmers, the urban poor and other vulnerable groups.

Policymakers need to ascertain that proposed policies are not evaluated in silos. Each has its unique impact on fiscal space and vulnerability; with the overall effect determined using a holistic approach. This will lead to a better prioritization of policies. A beneficial outcome requires a balance between macroeconomic stability and social progress. The historical experience of the PRC bodes well for the future.

APPENDIX: SUPPORT POLICY FOR MIGRANT WORKERS

Rural migrants are the largest group of migrant workers. Their basic needs are their children's education, employment, and housing, among others. Because the PRC lacks a systemic horizontal transfer payment system between provincial governments,[1] there are no statistics on transfers or tax revenues of migrant workers. Under fiscal decentralization, local governments have insufficient incentives to equalize the public services of migrant workers. Due to the institutional characteristics of "central government hosts a dinner party, while local governments pay the bills", there will be deviations in local government policy implementation. This appendix describes some key areas of policy support and preliminary policy results.

Education of Relocated Children of Migrant Workers

Educating the children of migrant workers is the most likely to induce social fragmentation, and is the most urgent issue they face. In the early 21st century, many migrant workers flooded into cities, leaving their children to be educated in rural areas due to the *hukuo* household registration system, and thus become "left-behind children"(留守儿童). Many of these left-behind children had psychological problems due to long-term lack of service and care from their parents, which also created other social issues.

To address this, the promulgation of the "Decision of the State Council on the Reform and Development of Basic Education"(State Council [2001])[2] at the beginning of the 21st century and the revision of the "Compulsory Education Law of the People's Republic of China" clarified the "two main body"[3] (两为主) guidelines. Follow-up policy measures continually propose to provide equal treatment for the education of relocated children. Starting from 2008, the central government has provided subsidies to local governments for the enrollment of children of eligible migrant workers in the compulsory education phase. However, their education depends largely on the importance attached by "in-flowing" or destination governments.

The "National New Urbanization Plan 2014–2020" required the in-flowing government to "incorporate compulsory education for relocated children of migrant workers into education development plans and fiscal security at all levels". Afterward, the education policy guidelines of relocated children of migrant workers changed from "two main body" to "two incorporations" (两纳入), which means to incorporate the permanent population into the regional education development plan, and incorporate the education of relocated children into the scope of fiscal expenditure responsibility.

---

1   Some scholars regard horizontal government aid and cross-provincial ecological compensation as horizontal transfer payments.
2   http://www.gov.cn/gongbao/content/2001/content_60920.htm.
3   The government of the inflowing region bears the main responsibility of compulsory education of the relocated children of migrant workers, and the public school bears the main responsibility of providing compulsory education for the relocated children of migrant workers.

Subsequently, the Ministry of Education and Ministry of Finance, along with other departments established a "uniform urban and rural compulsory education funding guarantee mechanism" to achieve "portable education funds" , or more succinctly, "money follows migrant". This portion has two components: (i) a standard quota for the shared expenses per student, and (ii) the "two exemptions and one supplementary fund" (mainly for tuition and miscellaneous fees for poor families, free textbooks, and subsidies for living expenses for boarders (寄宿生) with financial difficulties).

At the same time, to ensure the fairness of education, the Ministry of Education also requires simplifying the admission procedures for relocated children by mixing migrant and urban students when assigning classes.

The central government also provides incentives and support to provinces (mainly in eastern and central regions) to satisfy compulsory education requirements. In 2014, the central government invested CNY10.0 billion in incentives.[4] In addition, since 2014, the country also has begun implementing a "comprehensively renew schools with weak conditions (全面改薄)" policy to expand educational resources to meet the compulsory education enrollment needs of relocated children of migrant workers.

Since 2017, the monitoring report of migrant workers has begun publishing data on their education status. In 2017–2019, the kindergarten enrollment rate of relocated children 3–5 years old was 83.3%, 83.5%, and 85.8% respectively over the 3-years, with the school enrollment rate of migrant children in the compulsory education age 98.7%, 98.9% and 99.5%, respectively.

While this is positive from a statistical point of view, there remain many "pain points":

(i) under the fiscal decentralization system, although the central government guarantees the per capita educational fee of relocated children, the larger education costs go to expanding educational resources (to build new schools) and the increase in fiscal support for teachers and related administrative staff; (ii) although the central government demands simplified procedures, the materials required for enrolling in compulsory education for relocated children in large cities remain cumbersome. This invisible threshold creates two problems: on the one hand, many migrant workers leave their children to be educated in their hometowns, and maintain the status of left-behind children (this also explains why the data performs well); on the other hand, it is difficult to enter high quality public schools. Most of the time, only public schools and private schools in the suburbs with lower quality rankings open their doors. These schools have limited funds, poor schooling conditions, and insufficient enthusiasm among teachers. Finally, college entrance examinations are based on the place of household registration, with the test contents differing by province. Therefore, even if relocated children enjoy compulsory education in the city, for high school they must return to the place of household registration if they cannot get an urban identity in the city their parents work in.

Housing

If education is their greatest family concern, housing security is the primary concern of the workers themselves. In 2007, the central government issued the *"Guiding Opinions on Improving the Living Conditions of Rural Migrant Workers"*,[5] encouraging employers to construct collective dormitories in industrial parks for migrant workers, and encouraging residents in urban and rural combined areas (城乡结合部) to lease their own housing to migrant workers.

---

4   http://cppcc.people.com.cn/n/2015/0301/c34948-26615314.html.
5   http://www.mohurd.gov.cn/wjfb/200801/t20080110_157799.html.

The process of urbanization has rapidly increased the costs of commercial housing. Many urban low-income families cannot pay market rates, so there are many "floating populations" requiring urgent attention. The central government has put forward a policy to speed up public rental housing. In 2010, the Ministry of Housing and Urban-Rural Development issued its *"Guiding Opinions on Accelerating the Development of Public Rental Housing"*,[6] which stipulates that the supply of public rental housing should be for urban middle-income families with housing difficulties. It encourages qualified areas for new employees with stable occupations who have lived for a certain number of years within the urban housing system.

In 2011, the State Council issued its *"Guiding Opinions on the Construction and Management of Comfortable Housing Projects (安居工程)"*,[7] which proposed that the public rental housing system be an important way to manage an orderly migrant flow and promote healthy urbanization. The policy also said that, in developments and industrial parks where migrant workers are concentrated,

unit-type or dormitory-type public rental housing will be built, and be rented out to industrial park employers or employees. But according to the *2016 Peasant Workers Monitoring Report*, less than 3% of rural migrant workers can buy an affordable house or rent public rental houses. It reported that 62.4% of migrant workers rent private houses by themselves. These include informal housing (no property certification) located in "urban villages" (城中村), with many group renting.[8]

In recent years, urban village renovation and the remediation of group rents have compressed living spaces of migrant workers while increasing housing rent. Many local governments are trying to lower the threshold to apply for public rental housing, and expanding availability through urban renewal projects while reconstructing "urban villages".

From a statistical perspective, the living conditions of rural migrant workers have continued to improve in recent years, and per capita living space continues to increase (Figure A1.1). In 2019, 52.2% of rural migrant workers living in cities have

Figure A1.1: Per Capita Living Space of Rural Migrant Workers, 2014–2019
(square meters)

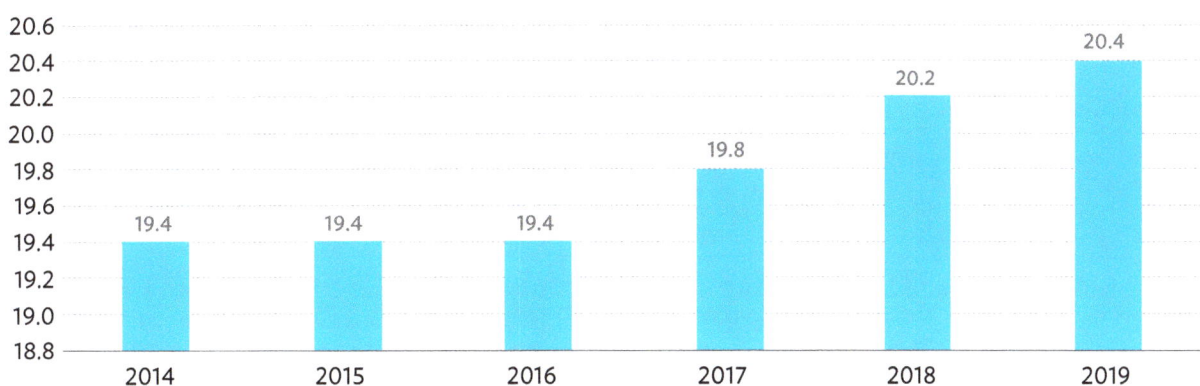

Source: National Bureau of Statistics. 2015–2020. 2014–2019 Peasant Workers Monitoring Report.

---

6   http://www.mohurd.gov.cn/wjfb/201006/t20100612_201308.html.
7   http://www.gov.cn/zhengce/content/2011-09/29/content_7236.htm.
8   Which refers to dividing apartments into smaller rooms and renting them separately. Group renting is not legal in China because it may cause fire problems and affect the normal lives of neighbors.

heating facilities; 83.7% have bathing facilities; 94.8% have internet access; with the share with refrigerators, washing machines, and automobiles (including business vehicles) at 65.7%, 66.1%, and 28.2% respectively.

Social Insurance

An important issue is social insurance. According to national regulations, employers and employees must pay "five insurances" when signing employment contracts. Among these, pension insurance, medical insurance and unemployment insurance are paid jointly by companies and individuals, with work injury insurance and maternity insurance borne by enterprises. Many companies also provide housing provident funds for employees (Table A1.1).

But the proportion of migrant workers participating in social insurance is very low. According to 2014 data, the actual participation of rural migrant workers is less than 20% (Table A1.2). This is because of the mismatch between the existing social insurance system and migrant worker needs. For example, in pension insurance, the insured person must accumulate 15 years of premiums before qualifying for retirement payments.

From the corporate perspective, paying social insurance increases costs directly, so many companies are reluctant to pay social insurance for rural migrant workers. From the perspective of migrant workers, paying social insurance directly affects their income, and the application process for social insurance is

Table A1.1: Proportion of Social Insurance Premiums and Housing Provident Funds Paid by Enterprises and Individuals

	Paid by Employer (%)	Paid by Employee (%)	Employer's Contribution Rate (%)
Pension	16	8	66.7
Medical	5–8	2	75.0
Unemployment	2	1	66.7
Work injury	1		100.0
Maternity	0.5–1		100.0
Housing provident funds	5-12	5-12	50.0

Note: Because the policy changes and policy incentives for various types of enterprises in different places differ, this form does not necessarily apply to all enterprises.
Source: Asian Development Bank.

Table A1.2: Proportion of Migrant Workers Participating in Social Insurance Housing Provident Fund in 2014
(%)

	Work Injury	Medical	Pension	Unemployment	Maternity	Housing Provident Fund
total	26.2	17.6	16.7	10.5	7.8	5.5
Rural migrant workers	29.7	18.2	16.4	9.8	7.1	5.6
Local peasant workers	21.1	16.8	17.2	11.5	8.7	5.3

Source: National Bureau of Statistics. 2015. 2014 Peasant Workers Monitoring Report.

cumbersome. Some migrant workers even refuse to accept employment because the company is responsible for social insurance.

However, this has recently changed. In 2009, the General Office of the State Council issued the Interim Measures for the Transfer and Continuation of Pension Insurance Relations for Enterprise Employees, realizing a smooth connection between the insured persons in the provincial overall planning area. In 2014, the Ministry of Human Resources and Social Security and the Ministry of Finance issued the Interim Measures for the Linkage of Urban and Rural Pension Insurance Systems, realizing the convergence between the basic pension insurance systems for enterprise employees and urban and rural residents. From 2019, the national taxation department and local taxation departments merged, with the collection of social insurance transferred from the former social insurance department to taxation departments. This led to more effective ways for enterprises to pay social insurance of migrant workers. At the same time, the PRC is trying to establish a portable social insurance information platform to make social insurance transfer more convenient and easier. The National Medical Insurance Bureau also strives to simplify the medical insurance reimbursement process for medical treatment, making the transfers of social insurance more convenient and fast.

However, it should also be pointed out that because many migrants are temporary or seasonal workers, employers often hire migrant workers through informal contracts or oral agreement. Also, some migrant workers do not have a fixed employer (such as babysitters) or are self-employed (in small restaurants or shops), which affects their ability to participate in employee social insurance schemes.

Employment Training

One important reason for the low-income dilemma of migrant workers is the general lack of skills. Therefore, employment training for migrant workers is also a key issue for the government. During 2014–2017, the government provided more than 38 million subsidized vocational skills training opportunities for migrant workers.[9] According to the "Peasant Workers Monitoring Report in 2017", 32.9% received agricultural and non-agricultural skills training, while 30.6% received non-agricultural skills training.

Problems include the small scale of training and targeted groups are not clearly defined. In 2019, the Ministry of Human Resources and Social Security issued the "New Generation Rural Migrant Worker Occupational Skills Upgrading Plan" (2019–2022), which proposed many new financial support methods, such as training vouchers, free participation in skills education and vocational training for the documented poor population, supporting enterprises for employee education and training, government subsidies to vocational colleges and training institutions, and expanding the scope of the government purchase training service. In the process of implementing local government policy, some local governments subsidize 30% of the training fee; and there are some local governments that provide free training for rural migrant workers by subsidizing training institutions. Meanwhile, a one-time employment subsidy is provided to those who have a 1-year or more official labor contract; they pay social insurance according to national regulations with local enterprises after completing the training program.

9   https://baijiahao.baidu.com/s?id=1625487674871571820&wfr=spider&for=pc.

Those Returning Home to Start a Business

Huge numbers of migrant workers have helped create urban prosperity. But they have also contributed to the phenomenon of "hollowing rural areas". Therefore, the PRC has always tried various methods to encourage rural migrant workers to return to their hometowns and start businesses. In 2015, the State Council initiated the *"Opinions on Supporting Rural Workers and Other Persons to Return to their Hometowns for Entrepreneurship"*. In May 2017, the General Office of the CCCPC issued *"Opinions on Accelerating the Construction of a Policy System to Train New Agricultural Business Entities"* to encourage and support emerging agricultural businesses. These policies have achieved good results. At the end of 2019, the number of entrepreneurs returning home exceeded 8.5 million, with on average, each entrepreneur returning home creating 4 new jobs.[10]

In 2019, the *"Opinions on Further Enhancing Entrepreneurial Work for Returning to Hometowns"* issued by the Ministry of Human Resources and Social Security, the Ministry of Finance, and the Ministry of Agriculture and Rural Affairs, expressed the need to further promote entrepreneurship of those returning to the countryside, promoting innovative businesses, urban-rural and inter-industrial integration. Fiscal policy tools include subsidies for entrepreneurship training, tax reductions, site arrangement policies, one-time entrepreneurial subsidies, social insurance subsidies, and access to secured loans. In the process of implementing these policies, local governments are also offering support, for example, in Xinyang City (信阳市), a southern city in Henan Province, which has a large migrant outflow. The policy requires that at least CNY10 million and CNY5 million should be allocated each year at the municipal and county levels, listed in the annual budget, and used for encouraging migrant workers to return home to start a business.

Response to COVID-19

The outbreak of COVID-19 had a huge impact on migrant workers. Many enterprises could not operate normally, and the demand for workers dropped sharply. A series of policy measures were issued to support migrant workers.

In March 2020, the *"Operation Opinions on Measures for Strengthening Employment and Stabilizing Employment in Response to the Impact of COVID-19"*[11] (State Council 2020b) issued by the General Office of the State Council, proposed three elements of support for the employment of migrant workers.

First, the government uses the method of providing "point to point" transportation for migrant workers, and promotes mutual recognition of health information between host and source regions,[12] At the same time, special vehicles, special trains, charter flights, among others provided arrangements for migrant workers to return to work as soon as possible. Organizing targeted labor cooperation through online recruitment activities also helped.

Second, migrant workers are encouraged to look for jobs nearby or in their hometown. Employment has been promoted by supporting industry development, establishing poverty alleviation workshops and encouraging business start-ups motivated by the ones returning home. A work-for relief project expands employment

---

[10]   http://www.xinhuanet.com/gongyi/2018-01/29/c_129798032.htm.
[11]   http://www.gov.cn/zhengce/content/2020-03/20/content_5493574.htm.
[12]   So migrant workers are not forced to quarantine for 14 days after returning to work.

channels for migrant workers. At the same time, many local governments also provide fiscal subsidies for workers returning to their hometowns. For example, in Chenzhou City (郴州市), Hunan Province, CNY800 per person subsidies are given to those who have been employed in local industrial parks for more than 6 months. Department of Human Resources and Social Welfare of Sichuan Province tried to match local enterprises with returning migrant workers by industry, region and level.

Third, incentives for employing rural migrant workers encourage enterprises to recruit more labor from poverty areas. The government also supports the employment of migrant workers by expanding the scale of public welfare positions in rural areas and enhancing online vocational skills training, among others.

And fourth, in May 2020, the Ministry of Human Resources and Social Security and the Ministry of Finance jointly issued the *Notice on Expanding the Coverage of Unemployment Insurance* (Ren She Bu Fa [2020] N0. 40) to gradually expand the coverage of migrant workers, and for those jobless migrant workers who have worked continuously for less than one year after 1 January 2019, with reference to the urban subsistence allowance standard, will be given monthly temporary living allowances of no more than 3 months. Unemployed migrant workers who participate in the insurance and pay the same fees as urban employees will be paid unemployment insurance or unemployment subsidies in accordance with the provisions of the place of insurance. The two subsidy policies complement each other and include all insured unemployed migrant workers in the scope of the system guarantee, effectively guaranteeing the basic livelihood of migrant workers during the critical period.

REFERENCES

Ahmad E., and Hans van Rijn. 2020. The Role of Local Governments in Driving High-Quality Growth in the People's Republic of China. Manila: ADB.

Ali, Ifzal, and Hyun H. Son. 2007. Defining and Measuring Inclusive Growth: Application to the Philippines. *ERD Working Paper Series* No. 98. Manila: ADB. p. 1–2.

Asian Development Bank (ADB). 2020a. Asia's Journey to Prosperity: Policy, Market, and Technology Over 50 Years. Manila: ADB.

————. 2020b. An Updated Assessment of the Economic Impact of COVID-19. *ADB BRIEFS*. No. 133. Manila:ADB. DOI: http://dx.doi.org/10.22617/BRF200144-2 (accessed 6 October 2020).

————. 2020c. *Observations and Suggestions: Post-2020 Poverty Reduction Policy Options for the People's Republic of China.* Manila.

Bingzhi, Han. 2019. "Strengthen vocational skills training for the new generation of migrant workers." *Economic Daily*, February 15. https://baijiahao.baidu.com/s?id=1625487674871571820&wfr=spider&for=pc (accessed October 8, 2020).

Cai, Yingqi, Jiayue Wang, and Liang Zhang. 2019. Journal of Central China Normal University (Humanities and Social Sciences), 58(05):25-37. (蔡迎旗,王佳悦,张亮.我国学前教育供给模式的演变历程与展望:1949—2019[J].华中师范大学学报(人文社会科学版), 2019,58(05):25-37).

CEIC. China Premium Database. www.ceic.com (accessed 22 July 2020).

Central Committee of the CPC (CCCPC) and State Council. 2015a. *No. 1 Central Document.* http://english.www.gov.cn/policies/latest_ releases/2015/02/02/content_281475048989652.htm (accessed 7 October 2020).

————. 2015b. *"Opinions on Speeding up the Construction of Ecological Civilization."* http://www.gov.cn/xinwen/2015-05/05/content_2857363. htm (accessed 7 October 2020).

————. 2018. *Policies released on China's rural vitalization.* http://english.www.gov.cn/ policies/latest_ releases/2018/02/04/content_281476035954734.htm (accessed 7 October 2020).

————. 2019. *Measures eye rural, urban integration.* http://english.www.gov.cn/policies/ policy_watch/2019/05/06/content_281476646637174.htm (accessed 7 October 2020).

Chen, S. and M. Ravallion. 2012. More Relatively-Poor People in a Less Absolutely-Poor World. *World Bank Policy Research Working Paper* 6114. Washington D.C.: World Bank. https://openknowledge. worldbank.org/bitstream/handle/10986/11876/WPS6114.pdf?sequence=1&isAllowed=y (accessed 8 October 2020).

Chengdu Municipal People's Government. 2018. *"Opinions of the General Office of the Chengdu Municipal People's Government on Further Improving the Basic Pension Service Subsidy System for the Elderly."* (accessed 27 November 2020).

China Development Research Foundation. 2017. China REACH: Final Evaluation Report on Project in Huachi County, Gansu Province. (中国发展研究基金会, 2017, 慧育中国：甘肃华池县项目终期评估报告).

China Education Yearbook. 1979-2018. Number of Kindergarten (Forage 3-6) in PRC (1979-2018).

————. 1979-2018. Percentage chart by kindergarten providers in PRC (1979-2018).

China Environmental Bulletin. 2007-2018.

China Statistical Yearbook. Annual disposable income of urban and rural residents (yuan), 2003-3028. https://data.stats.gov.cn/easyquery.htm?cn=C01 (accessed 8 October 2020).

————. Main Durable Goods Owned Per 100 Rural Households, 2006 and 2016. https://data.stats.gov.cn/ easyquery.htm?cn=C01 (accessed 8 October 2020).

————. Rural tourism and domestic tourism in 2012-2018. https://data.stats.gov.cn/ easyquery. htm?cn=C01 (accessed 8 October 2020).

————. Share of rural tourism in total tourism, 2012-2018. https://data.stats.gov.cn/ easyquery. htm?cn=C01 (accessed 8 October 2020).

China Yearbook of Household Survey. 2019. Annual disposable income per capita of rural residents by income group (yuan), 2005, 2008, 2011, 2014, 2017, 2018. http://cdi.cnki.net/Titles/ SingleNJ?NJCode=N2013120091 (accessed 8 October 2020).

————. Total rural workers and number of migrant workers. https://data.cnki.net/yearbook/Single/ N2019120179 (accessed 8 June 2020).

Employment and Social Development Canada, Government of Canada. 2018. Canadian Poverty Reduction Strategy. https://www.canada.ca/en/employment-social-development/programs/poverty-reduction. html (accessed 15 October 2020).

Evans, David, and Mead Over. (12 March 2020). The Economic Impact of COVID-19 in Low- and MiddleIncome Countries. Blog in Center for Global Development. https://www.cgdev.org/blog/ economicimpact-covid-19-low-and-middle-income-countries (accessed 12 October 2020).

Fan, Shenggen., Wei Si, and Yumei Zhang. 2020. "How to prevent a global food and nutrition security crisis under COVID-19?" *China Agricultural Economic Review*, Volume 12 Issue 3.

Fan, Shenggen and Yumei Zhang. 2021 (mimeo). Impact of COVID-19 on Food Supply Chains, Rural Migrants and Poverty in the People's Republic of China. Forthcoming in *ADB East Asian Working Paper Series*. Manila: ADB.

Gallardo, Mauricio. 2018. "Identifying Vulnerability To Poverty: A Critical Survey," *Journal of Economic Surveys*, Wiley Blackwell, vol. 32(4), pages 1074-1105, September. (accessed 9 October 2020).

Gao, R., B. Cao, Y. Hu, Z. Feng, D. Wang, W. Hu, J. Chen et al. 2013. "Human Infection with a Novel AvianOrigin Influenza A (H7N9) Virus." *The New England Journal of Medicine* 368:1888-1897. DOI: 10.1056/NEJMoa1304459 (accessed 6 October 2020).

Glawe, Linda, and Helmut Wagner. 2017. The People's Republic of China in the Middle-Income Trap? *ADBI Working Paper* No. 749. Tokyo: Asian Development Bank Institute. https://www.adb.org/publications/ prc-middle-income-trap (accessed 6 October 2020).

Global Times. "China spends $2,395 on average for each COVID-19 patient." *Global Times*, March 29, 2020. https://www.globaltimes.cn/content/1184060.shtml (accessed 6 October 2020).

Golley, Jane, Yixiao Zhou, and Meiyan Wang. 2019. Inequality of Opportunity in China's Labor Earnings: The Gender Dimension. China & World Economy: 27 (1): 28-50. https://doi.org/10.1111/cwe.12266 (accessed 6 October 2020).

Guo, Ruliang, Liu Ziyu and Chen Jianghua. 2020. Part-time farming, land fragmentation, and socialized agricultural machinery services: A case study of Jiangxi Province. *Research of Agricultural Modernization*, No.1:135-143 [in Chinese]. DOI: 10.13872/j.1000-0275.2019.0108 (accessed 9 October 2020).

Gustafsson, Björn, and Sai Ding. 2019 . Growing Into Relative Income Poverty: Urban China 1988 to 2013. *Discussion Paper Series*, Issue 12422, Forschungsinstitut zur Zukunft der Arbeit. IZA - Institute of Labor Economics.

Habib, Najibullah. "Protecting vulnerable groups— sector perspectives: Implications for Health in the People's Republic of China." Unpublished manuscript. April 2020.

Habib, Najibullah, Stefan Rau, Susann Roth, Felipe Silva, and Janis Shandro. 2020. Healthy and Age-Friendly Cities in the People's Republic Of China, Proposal for Health Impact Assessment and Healthy and Age-Friendly City Action and Management Planning. Manila: ADB.

Hangzhou Municipal Civil Affairs Bureau and Hangzhou Municipal Finance Bureau. 2019. "Methods for implementing subsidies for EC services in Hangzhou", http://www.hangzhou.gov.cn/art/2019/4/1/art_1636467_4550.html (accessed 9 October 2020).

Haughton, Jonathan, and Shahidur R. Khandker.2009. Handbook on Poverty and Inequality. Washington, DC: World Bank. https://openknowledge.worldbank.org/handle/10986/11985 License: CC BY 3.0 IGO. http://hdl.handle.net/10986/11985 (accessed 12 October 2020).

Hoddinott, John, and Agnes Quisumbing. 2010. Methods for Microeconometric Risk and Vulnerability Assessment. In: Fuentes-Nieva R., Seck P.A. (eds) Risk, Shocks, and Human Development. Palgrave Macmillan, London. https://doi.org/10.1057/9780230274129_4 (accessed 12 October 2020).

Honda, Jiro, and Hiroaki Miyamoto. 2020. Would Population Aging Change the Output Effects of Fiscal Policy? *IMF Working Paper* WP/20/92. (accessed 9 October 2020)

Hongzhi, Cui. 2020. "Improving the Social Security System Covering the Rural Population: Current Situation, Problems and Suggestions." *Journal of Xinjiang Normal University (Edition of Philosophy and Social Sciences)*, No.5: 18-28 [in Chinese]. https://doi.org/10.14100/j.cnki.65-1039/g4.20200307.001 (accessed 16 October 2020)

Huang, Yanzhong. 2004. SARS Epidemic and its aftermath in China: A Political Perspective. Adapted from The Politics of China's SARS Crisis. *Harvard Asia Quarterly* (Autumn 2003). National Academy of Sciences. https://www.ncbi.nlm.nih.gov/books/NBK92479/ (accessed 9 October 2020).

International Labour Organization. 2020. Social protection responses to the Covid-19 crisis: Country responses in Asia and the Pacific. *ILO Brief*. ILO: Geneva. https://www.ilo.org/wcmsp5/groups/public/--asia/---ro-bangkok/documents/briefingnote/wcms_739587.pdf (accessed 9 October 2020).

International Monetary Fund. 2019. Macroeconomics of Aging and Policy Implications. Washington D.C.: International Monetary Fund.

Keqiang, Li. 2020. *Government Work Report (On-site Record) at the Third Session of the Thirteenth National People's Congress on May 22, 2020*. http://www.cpad.gov.cn/art/2020/5/22/art_61_123261.html (accessed 12 October 2020).

Kimura, Shingo, Wusheng Yu, and Mingxi Han. 2021 (mimeo). Multidimensional evolution of PRC's rural development policy: Lessons for Developing Asia. Forthcoming in *ADB East Asian Working Paper Series*. Manila: ADB.

Labonté, Ronald, Abdullahel Hadi, and Xaxier Kauffmann. 2011. Indicators of Social Exclusion and Inclusion: A Critical and Comparative Analysis of the Literature. EI Exchange Working Paper Series, Volume 2, Number 8.

Lagarde, Christine, and Erna Solberg. 2018. "Why 2018 must be the year for women to thrive." *World Economic Forum*. https://www.weforum.org/agenda/2018/01/the-time-has-come-for-women-tothrive-heres-how/ (accessed 12 October 2020).

Lee, Minsoo, Joon-Kyung Kim, Myung Ho Park, Longyun Peng, Tetsuji Okazaki, and Susumu Ishii. 2020. Developing Modernization Indicators for the People's Republic of China: Key Considerations and a Proposed Framework. Manila: ADB.

Li, Jiangyi. 2020. "The Effect of Land Entitlement on Non-agricultural Labor Participation." *Economic Science*, No.1: 113-126 [in Chinese].

Li, Shi, Peng Zhan, and Yangyang Shen. 2020. New Patterns in China's Rural Poverty. In T. Sicular, S. Li, X. Yue and H. Sato, eds. *Changing Trends in China's Inequality: Evidence, Analysis, and Prospects*. New York: Oxford University Press. DOI:10.1093/oso/9780190077938.001.0001 (accessed 12 October 2020).

Lijuan, Pang, Wang Honglei, Ji Dongying, Yuan Qiuhong, and He Hongfang. 2019. "The Effective Policies to Construct an Education and Care System for the 0–3 Year-Old Children in China." *Journal of Beijing Normal University (Social Sciences)*, Vol 06:5-11. (庞丽娟,王红蕾,冀东莹,袁秋红,贺红芳.有效构建我国0—3岁婴幼儿教保服务体系的政策思考[J].北京师范大学学报(社会科学版),2019(06):5-11.)

Liu, Ying. 2019. Is the Distribution of Early Childhood Education Financial Resources Between Rural and Urban China More Equal? The Progress of the Vertical Equity in Chinese ECE Fiscal System Since 2010. *Forum on Contemporary Education*, Vol 5:54-57. (刘颖.城乡学前教育财政经费分配更公平了吗?—2010年来我国城乡学前教育财政公平的进展[J]. 当代教育论坛, 2019 (05):17-24.)

Marchisio, Matteo. "The impact of COVID-19 on smallholders in China." *China's Poverty Reduction Online*, June 1, 2020. http://p.china.org.cn/2020-06/01/content_76114092.htm (accessed 13 October 2020).

Martin, V., DU Pfeiffer, X. Zhou, X. Xiao X, DJ Prosser, F. Guo, M. Gilbert. 2011. "Spatial Distribution and RiskFfactors of Highly Pathogenic Avian Influenza (HPAI) H5N1 in China." *PLoS Pathog* 7(3): e1001308. https://doi.org/10.1371/journal.ppat.1001308 (accessed 14 October 2020).

Ministry of Agriculture and Rural Affairs. 2015. 2020 Zero-Growth Action Plan for Chemical Fertilizers and Pesticides. http://www.moa.gov.cn/ztzl/mywrfz/gzgh/201509/t20150914_4827907.htm (accessed 13 October 2020).

Ministry of Civil Affairs (MCA). 2017. Statistical Bulletin of Social Service Development. http://www.mca. gov.cn/article/sj/tjgb/2017/201708021607.pdf (accessed 14 October 2020).

———. 2019. Statistical Communiqué of Social Service Development in 2018. http://images3.mca.gov.cn/ www2017/file/201908/1565920301578.pdf (accessed 14 April 2020).

———. 2020. Statistical Bulletin of Social Service Development, http://images3.mca.gov.cn/www2017/ file/202009/1601261242921.pdf (accessed 14 October 2020).

Ministry of Ecology and Environment. 2020. Implementation of the 2019 Water Pollution Prevention and Control Action Plan. http://www.gov.cn/xinwen/2020-05/17/content_5512338.htm (accessed 13 October 2020).

Ministry of Finance, Ministry of Civil Affairs and National Office on Aging. 2014. "Circular on providing subsidies for old people with advanced age and financial difficulties." http://www.gov.cn/ xinwen/2014-10/23/content_2769678.htm (accessed 14 October 2020).

Ministry of Human Resources and Social Security. 2016. *"Guiding Opinions of the General Office of the Ministry of Human Resources and Social Security on the Pilot Long-term Care Insurance System."* http://www.gov.cn/xinwen/2016-07/08/content_5089283.htm (accessed 14 April 2020).

National Bureau of Statistics (NBS). Gross Domestic Product Growth, 1998-2018. http://www.stats.gov.cn/tjsj/ndsj/2018/indexeh.htm (accessed 31 August 2019).

————. 2000–2019. Poverty Monitoring Report of Rural China. Beijing: China Statistical Press.

————. 2015–2020. 2014–2019 Peasant Workers Monitoring Report.

————. 2017. Third National Agricultural Census. Rural transportation facilities, Rural energy and communication facilities, Rural household sanitary facilities. http://www.stats.gov.cn/tjsj/tjgb/nypcgb/ qgnypcgb/ (accessed 15 October 2020).

————. 2020. 2019 National migrant survey report. http://www.stats.gov.cn/ tjsj/zxfb/202004/t20200430_1742724.html (accessed 2 June 2020).

National Development and Reform Commission. 2016. "Circular on methods of providing central subsidies for supporting EC development", http:// www.gov.cn/xinwen/2016-12/30/content_5154994.htm (accessed 15 April 2020).

National Healthcare Security Administration. 2020. "Statistical Communique for development of basic medical care security system in 2019", http://www.nhsa.gov.cn/ art/2020/6/24/art_7_3268.html (accessed 11 January 2021).

National People's Congress. 1956. Model Charter of Agricultural Production Cooperatives. http://www.npc.gov.cn/wxzl/ wxzl/2000-12/10/content_4304.htm (accessed 15 October 2020).

————. 2004. Agricultural Mechanization Promotion Law. http://www.gov.cn/gongbao/content/2004/ content_72367.htm (accessed 15 October 2020).

Prosser, DJ, P. Cui, JY Takekawa, M. Tang, Y. Hou, BM Collins, B. Yan et al. 2011. "Wild Bird Migration across the Qinghai-Tibetan Plateau: A Transmission Route for Highly Pathogenic H5N1." *PLoS ONE* 6(3): e17622. https://doi.org/10.1371/journal.pone.0017622 (accessed 16 October 2020).

Qin, Amy. "Stop Asking Women About Childbearing Status, China Tells Employers." *The New York Times*, February 21, 2019. https://www.nytimes.com/2019/02/21/world/china-gender-discriminationworkplace.html (accessed 16 October 2020).

Shi, Zhengli, and Zhihong Hu. 2008. "A review of studies on animal reservoirs of the SARS coronavirus." Virus Research 2008;133: 74–87. doi:10.1016/j.virusres.2007.03.012 (Available online 23 April 2007) (accessed 16 October 2020).

Song, Yingquan. 2019. Principal Contradictions and Reformation of Public Finance in Early Childhood Education and Care in China. *China Economics of Education Review*, Vol 3:19-48. (宋映泉.我国学前教育事业发展主要矛盾与公共财政投入改革方向[J].教育经济评论, 2019,4(03):19-48.)

State Administration for Industry and Commerce. Number of Professional Farmer Cooperatives. http:// gkml.samr.gov.cn/index.html?gkml=gknb (accessed 14 October 2020).

State Council. Bulletin No. 23, 2001. Decision of the State Council on the Reform and Development of Basic Education. http://www.gov.cn/gongbao/content/2001/content_60920.htm (accessed 14 October 2020).

———. 2010. *"Opinions on encouraging and guiding private capital to enter the EC service industry"*; MCA (2012) *"Opinions on implementing policies for encouraging and guiding private capital to enter the EC service industry"*, http://www.gov.cn/zhengce/2016-05/22/content_5075659. htm (accessed 14 April 2020).

———. 2011. *"Guiding Opinions of the General Office of the State Council on the Construction and Management of Affordable Housing Projects."* http://www.gov.cn/zhengce/ content/2011-09/29/content_7236.htm (accessed 14 October 2020).

———. 2015. *"Several Opinions of the General Office of the State Council on Further Promoting Tourism Investment and Consumption."* http://www.gov.cn/zhengce/content/2015-08/11/ content_10075.htm (accessed 14 October 2020).

———. 2019. Report on the development of rural industries. http://www.npc.gov.cn/npc/c30834/20 1904/1e30cb31a2a242cdb82586c5510f756d.shtml (accessed 14 October 2020).

———. 2020a. More subsidies soon for at-risk groups. http://english.www.gov.cn/statecouncil/ ministries/202004/11/content_WS5e91252bc6d0c201c2cc0abe.html (accessed 28 August 2020)

———. 2020b. *"Operation Opinions on Measures for Strengthening Employment and Stabilizing Employment in Response to the Impact of COVID-19."* http://www.gov.cn/zhengce/content/2020-03/20/ content_5493574.htm (accessed 14 October 2020).

———. 2020c. *2020 Zero Poverty: Briefing on securing the timely delivery of poverty alleviation goals. China Global Television Network*, March 12. Beijing. https://news.cgtn.com/ news/2020-03-12/China-confident-in-triumph-against-poverty-despite-COVID-19-impactONgHpPHGZq/index.html (accessed 15 October 2020).

Stiglitz, J. E. 2012. The Price of Inequality. New York: W. W. Norton and Company, Inc. UNDESA 2018, Chapter V.

Tencent Education. 2017. White Book of Childcare Service Industry in China. https://new.qq.com/ omn/20171206/20171206A0OKRI.html (腾讯教育, 2017, 中国0-3岁儿童托育服务行业白皮书) (accessed 16 October 2020).

Terada-Hagiwara, Akiko, Park Donghyun, and Hans van Rijn. 2018. Three Features of Aging in the People's Republic of China and Implications for Development Agenda. ADB Briefs No. 103. Manila: ADB.

Tong, Liu, and Yi Nie. (2008). Interpretation of American Head Start Program Performance Standards on Parent Involvement. *Studies in Early Childhood Education*, Vol 09:54-57. (刘彤,聂懿.解读美国开端计划家长参与执行标准[J].学前教育研究, 2008(09):54-57).

United Nations. 2018. *The World's Cities in 2018: Data Booklet*, Statistical Papers - United Nations (Ser. A), Population and Vital Statistics Report, UN, New York. https://doi.org/10.18356/c93f4dc6-en (accessed 13 October 2020).

United Nations, Department of Economic and Social Affairs, Population Division. 2019. World Population Prospects 2019, custom data acquired via https://population.un.org/wpp/DataQuery/ (accessed 13 October 2020).

United Nations Economic and Social Commission for Asia and the Pacific. 2018. Social Outlook for Asia and the Pacific: Poorly Protected. Reprint, Bangkok: 2019. https://www.unescap.org/sites/default/files/publications/SDD-SP-Social-Outlook-v14-1-E.pdf (accessed 20 November 2020)

Wang, CJ, H. Xiang, DR Liu, JJ He, and SF Nie. 2007. "Reflection on legal construction of Chinese public health emergencies." *Med Soc*, 20:38–40.

Wang L., Y. Wang, S. Jin, Z. Wu, D. Chin, J. Koplan, and E. Wilson. 2008. "Emergence and control of infectious diseases in China." *The Lancet* 372(9649):1598-605. https://doi.org/10.1016/S01406736(08)61365-3 (accessed 13 October 2020).

Wei, Ha. 2021 (mimeo). Early Childhood Development and Poverty Reduction in the People's Republic of China. *ADB East Asian Working Paper Series*. Manila: Asian Development Bank.

Wilder-Smith, A., and DO. Freedman. 2020. "Isolation, quarantine, social distancing and community containment: pivotal role for old-style public health measures in the novel coronavirus (2019-nCoV) outbreak." *Journal of Travel Medicine*, 27(2): taaa020. https://doi.org/10.1093/jtm/taaa020 (accessed 13 October 2020).

World Bank. 2020. Poverty and Equity Brief: China. https://databank.worldbank.org/data/download/poverty/987B9C90-CB9F-4D93-AE8C-750588BF00QA/AM2020/Global_POVEQ_CHN.pdf (accessed 16 October 2020).

———. Poverty and Equity Data Portal. http://povertydata.worldbank.org/poverty/country/CHN (accessed 21 April 2020).

World Bank, and the Development Research Center of the State Council, P. R. China. 2013. China 2030: Building a Modern, Harmonious, and Creative Society. Washington, DC: World Bank. https://www. worldbank.org/content/dam/Worldbank/document/China-2030-complete.pdf.

World Health Organization (WHO) Regional Office for the Western Pacific and Asia Pacific Observatory on Health Systems and Policies. 2015. People's Republic of China health system review. Manila : WHO Regional Office for the Western Pacific. Health systems in transition vol.5, no.7, xxiii, 217 p. http://iris.wpro.who.int/handle/10665.1/11408 (accessed 12 October 2020).

————. 2016. International Health Regulation (2005) Third edition. https://www.who.int/ihr/publications/9789241580496/en/ (accessed 12 October 2020).

————. 2017. Asia Pacific Strategy for Emerging Diseases and Public Health Emergencies (APSED III): Advancing implementation of the International Health Regulations (2005). Manila, Philippines. World Health Organization Regional Office for the Western Pacific; 2017. Licence: CC BY-NC-SA 3.0 IGO.

————. 2020. *Novel coronavirus (2019-nCoV): Situation Report - 1*. Geneva: World Health Organization. January 21. https://www.who.int/docs/default-source/coronaviruse/situation-reports/20200121sitrep-1-2019-ncov.pdf?sfvrsn=20a99c10_4 (accessed 12 October 2020).

Wu, Jinhua, and Guangdong Provincial Department of Finance. 2021 (mimeo). Guangdong's Experience in Poverty Reduction. Forthcoming in *ADB East Asian Working Paper Series*. Manila: ADB.

Wu, Zunyou, and Jennifer McGoogan. 2020. "Characteristics of and Important Lessons From the Coronavirus Disease 2019 (COVID-19) Outbreak in China: Summary of a Report of 72 314 Cases From the Chinese Center for Disease Control and Prevention." *Journal of American Medical Association Network*. https://doi:10.1001/jama.2020.2648 (https://jamanetwork.com/journals/jama/fullarticle/2762130) (accessed 9 October 2020).

Wuhan Municipal Civil Affairs Bureau. 2017. *"Opinions on increasing supply of and speeding up EC services."* http://mzj.wuhan.gov.cn/zwgk_918/fdzdgk/ggfw/shfl/201708/t20170823_1000655.shtml (accessed 16 October 2020).

————. 2018. "Notice on Implementing Wuhan Municipality's Pension Service Subsidies for the Elderly in Special Needs" (accessed 27 November 2020).

Xi Jinping. 2017. "Decisive victory to build a well-off society in an all-round way and win the great victory of socialism with Chinese characteristics in the new era." Report at the 19th National Congress of the Communist Party of China. 18 October. http://cpc.people.com.cn/n1/2017/1028/c64094-29613660.html (accessed 28 October 2020).

Xia, Q. J., L. N. Song, and A. Simon. 2007. "Trends and Patterns of Urban Poverty in China:1988-2002." Economic Research Journal, No.9:96-111 [in Chinese].

Xiao, Haixiang and Hunan Provincial Department of Finance. 2021 (mimeo). Poverty Reduction and Sustainable Development - Hunan Case. Forthcoming in ADB East *Asian Working Paper Series*. Manila: ADB.

Xiaohui, Wang. 2020. "China Development Report: Trends of Population Aging and Policies." China Times, 26 June. http://finance.ifeng.com/c/7xcyp7HB6QV (accessed 20 October 2020).

Xiwen, Wang. 2018. "The employment effect of migrant workers returning to their hometowns to start a business is increasingly prominent" *Xinhuanet/Charity News*, January 29. http://www.xinhuanet.com/gongyi/2018-01/29/c_129798032.htm (accessed 9 October 2020).

Xu, Yuebin. 2021 (mimeo). Development and Performance of the Elderly Care System in the People's Republic of China: Evidence from Several Cities. Forthcoming in *ADB East Asian Working Paper Series*. Manila: ADB.

Yoshino, N., and H. Miyamoto. 2017. Declined Effectiveness of Fiscal and Monetary Policies Faced with Aging Population in Japan. *ADBI Working Paper* 691. Tokyo: Asian Development Bank Institute. https://www.adb.org/publications/decreased-effectiveness-fiscalmonetary-policies-japan-agingsociety (accessed October 12, 2020).

Yoshino, Naoyuki, Akiko Terada-Hagiwara and Hiroaki Miyamoto. 2021 (mimeo). Revisit Public Debt Stability Condition: Rethinking of the Domar Condition and Application to PRC Bond Market. Forthcoming in *ADB East Asian Working Paper Series*. Manila: ADB.

Yue, Jinglun, and Fan Xin. 2018. Childcare policy in China: Review, Reflection and Reconstruction. Social Sciences in China Vol 9: 92-111+206. (岳经纶,范昕.中国儿童照顾政策体系:回顾、反思与重构[J].中国社会科学, 2018(09):92-111+206)

Zeng, Xiaodong, and Fan Xin. 2009. Preschool Education's Fiscal System Reform in China during the Past 60 Years since the Founding of PRC. *Early Childhood Education*, Vol 30:1-5. (曾晓东,范昕.建国60年来我国学前教育财政制度改革研究[J].幼儿教育, 2009 (30):1-5.)

Zhang, Liying. 2017. "The study on childcare organization in early New China (1949-1959)." PhD Dissertation. Shanxi Normal University. (张丽英. 新中国初期托儿组织研究 (1949-1959)[D]. 山西师范大学, 2017.)

Zhang, Manlin. 2009. "Study on governance of farmers' specialized cooperatives in China." PhD Dissertation. Beijing Forestry University [in Chinese].

Zhang, Tiwei and Provincial Poverty Reduction Case Research Group of Yunnan Provincial Department of Finance. (unpublished). The Achievements and Experience of Poverty Alleviation in Yunnan Province. 2021.

Zhang, Y., X. Diao and K. Chen. 2021. "The Impact of COVID-19 on Migrants, Remittances, Household Incomes and Poverty in China: A Microsimulation Analysis." Manuscript submitted to China and World Economy for publication. 2020.

Zhang, Yumei, Xinshen Diao, Kevin Chen, Sherman Robinson and Shenggen Fan. 2020. "Impact of COVID-19 on China's macroeconomy and agri-food system – an economy-wide multiplier model analysis." *China Agricultural Economic Review*, Vol. 12 No. 3, pp. 387-407. https://doi.org/10.1108/ CAER-04-2020-0063 (accessed October 7, 2020).

Zhang, Zoey Ye. "China is Relaxing *Hukou* Restrictions in Small and Medium-Sized Cities." *China Briefing*, April 17, 2019. https://www.china-briefing.com/news/china-relaxing-*hukou*-restrictions-smallmedium-sized-cities/ (accessed 9 October 2020).

Zhao, Binyu. 2020. "China's authorities provide financial support for poverty alleviation in areas impacted by epidemic." *China's Poverty Reduction Online.* http://p.china.org.cn/2020-02/25/content_75742765.htm (accessed 7 October 2020).

Zhao, Guoqin. "Demystifying China's Fiscal System: under the Perspective of Fiscal Sustainability." Unpublished manuscript, July 2020a.

————. Policy Support for Migrant Workers under China`s Fiscal Decentralization System -History, Current Status and Future Tendency." Unpublished manuscript, June 2020b.

Zheng, Lingyi, Jianfei Luo, and Ganlin Hong. 2019. "The 70-year Historical Evolution and Development Orientation of Rural Basic Management System in New China: Based on the Interaction Between Rural Land Institutional Reform and Agricultural Management System Reform." *China Land Science,* No.12: 10-17 [in Chinese].

Zhu, N, Zhang D, Wang W, et al. 2020. A novel coronavirus from patients with pneumonia in China. 2019. *The New England Journal of Medicine*; 382: 727–33. https://www.nejm.org/doi/full/10.1056/nejmoa2001017 (accessed 12 October 2020).

www.ingramcontent.com/pod-product-compliance
Lightning Source LLC
Chambersburg PA
CBHW050047220326
41599CB00045B/7311